Burgess Sport Teaching Series

TEACHING BADMINTON

Ralph B. Ballou

Middle Tennessee State University
Murfreesboro, Tennessee

 Burgess Publishing Company
Minneapolis, Minnesota

Editorial: Wayne Schotanus, Anne Heller
Copy editor: Kathleen A. Michels
Art coordinator: Melinda Berndt
Cover design: Melinda Berndt
Compositor: Gloria Otremba

© 1982 by Burgess Publishing Company
Printed in the United States of America
Library of Congress Catalog Card Number 81-68519
ISBN 0-8087-4068-7

Burgess Publishing Company
7108 Ohms Lane
Minneapolis, Minnesota 55435

J I H G F E D C B A

Contents

Acknowledgments

Just as individual effort alone seldom is sufficient to complete any worthwhile task, so too is an acknowledgment seldom sufficient to compensate those individuals who assist in its completion. I am deeply indebted to Robert D. Clayton, Ed. D., for editing the manuscript and providing many excellent suggestions and general counsel; to Sandy Robert for taking photographs, typing the bulk of the initial drafts and offering constructive criticism; to graduate students Cheryl Lutz and Vicki Pless for serving as models; and to Wilma Grant for typing the balance of the original material and the final draft. I also wish to thank my wife Phyllis for her valuable advice and support and my family for their patience.

A special note of thanks is extended to Cletus Eli, secretary-treasurer of the United States Badminton Association, for allowing the reproduction of material from the *Official Rules of Play*. Also, A. S. Barnes & Company, Inc., permitted me to reproduce material from *Winning Badminton* (Copyright © 1953 by Kenneth R. Davidson and Lealand R. Gustavson, all rights reserved).

1

Introduction

To be most effective, teaching and learning require an environment that stimulates the teacher to present the subject in the best possible way and the student to become as proficient as possible. Unfortunately, the development of sports skills is often difficult because of limitations imposed by the adequacy of the teaching facility and equipment, the size of the class, the time available, and the attitude and experience of the teacher.

Although many activity texts are written to help physical education teachers and students perform specific skills, few are devoted to the teaching of those skills. This text prepares the beginning teacher with a limited badminton background to teach a badminton unit with confidence. Thus, it serves as a teaching guide and as a text for physical education methods classes. Although this text presents various techniques and concepts for consideration by beginning and experienced teachers, it acknowledges that no one approach is ever absolute.

Teaching, to be successful, must begin at the student's level of expertise in the sport. For the purposes of this text, it is presumed that the beginning student has little or no experience playing badminton. Modifications are suggested for classes with students of mixed abilities. Making the class presentation concise and positive is emphasized. A deliberate effort has been made to describe each skill in language that will enable the teacher to communicate effectively with all students regardless of their handedness. Also, because a sport is more than just a series of skills, the beginning sequence of lessons includes some background on the development of badminton as a sport. Finally, this text provides the teacher with an extensive list of articles, texts, and evaluation material.

2

Course Objectives

A badminton class is more than a series of isolated skills. Indeed, a badminton class can help the student develop lasting friendships, improve his or her physical skills, and integrate individual skills into a complete game. Furthermore, the class can influence the student's attitude toward badminton in particular and promote an appreciation of a lifetime of physical activity in general.

Such potential depends on many factors: the teaching skill of the instructor, the adequacy of the facility and equipment, the time spent on instruction and practice, the aspirations of the student, and the objectives of the course. This chapter discusses course objectives, stressing that they should be comprehensive and written in behavioral terms.

EDUCATIONAL DOMAINS

According to current thought in education, learning occurs in three domains (or areas):

1. Affective—development or modification of the student's values, attitudes, appreciation, and aesthetic tastes. Because these factors do not lend themselves to objective assessment, evaluation is difficult, most often being done by observation on the part of the teacher.
2. Cognitive—learning of rules, strategy, verbalization of techniques, and definitions of specific shots and terms. Evaluation is most often conducted by means of written or oral examinations.
3. Psychomotor—performance of activity skills. The end result is the degree to which the student is able to integrate the component parts of each aspect of the activity into a fluid movement. Because evaluation is conducted by means of objective performance tests, this area is easier to assess than the affective and cognitive domains.

To achieve any measure of success, a course must have stability and a sense of direction. Course objectives should be written to set the course's direction and tone. Unit objectives for the lessons are then derived from course objectives. At the conclusion of the course, evaluation is done to determine whether or not course objectives have been met. If objectives have not been reached, they must be modified before the course is taught again.

BEHAVIORAL OBJECTIVES

Objectives written in terms of the affective, cognitive, and psychomotor educational domains serve as a blueprint or a plan of action for both teacher and student. Behavioral objectives are advocated; when well written, they state the precise behavior to be demonstrated, the point in the course when the behavior will be demonstrated, and the level of competence required. The standards set for the student should be realistic in relation to the time available to meet the objectives and the student's initial level of expertise. Although not a true behavioral objective, the percentage of the class that should have attained the competency standard by the end of the course is included in the following material.

The objectives set forth below cover a three-level sequence: beginning, intermediate, and advanced. When only one level is taught, the instructor must choose the objectives that best suit the situation. Class structure should be based on the experiential background of the students. Teachers working in agencies (e.g., YMCA, YWCA, recreation centers) can use the selective process to build a class unless a specific group must be taught.

Beginning Level Course Objectives

Even though one of the three domains may be emphasized more at one level than another, each domain should be represented at all levels of instruction. Beginning instruction should cover the basic strokes and shots, the basic rules and strategy for elementary singles and doubles play, and the development of an appreciation of the sport as a lifetime activity to be played either on a competitive or recreational basis.

Affective Domain

Evaluation in the affective domain, although very difficult and sometimes not even considered, usually is done by the instructor observing the student's behavior. At the conclusion of the course, 75% of beginning students should:

1. Appreciate the value of a partner in doubles play, e.g., talking to the instructor about the way they as a team will play.
2. Appreciate badminton as a lifetime activity, e.g., playing at least once in an intramural game or during leisure time or coming early to class or remaining after class.
3. Respect the skills of each partner, e.g., not encroaching on his or her territory to make a play.
4. Use proper etiquette, e.g., shaking hands and introducing themselves to each other before playing a game and shaking hands afterward.
5. Understand the need to keep the equipment in good condition, e.g., properly storing rackets, shuttles, and nets.

Cognitive Domain

Most activity classes have one or two written or oral examinations that enable the student to display the knowledge he or she has gained. Seventy-five percent or more of beginning students should score a minimum of 75% on such examinations, which should be given at midsemester or near the end of the course. Questions should test the student's knowledge of the:

1. Height of the net at center court and at the posts
2. Length of the court

3. Width of a singles court and a doubles court
4. Name of the estate for which the sport is named, the estate owner's name, and the village in which the estate is located
5. Name of the international team championships for men and women
6. Basic rules pertaining to serving and receiving
7. Service procedures in singles and doubles play
8. Definitions and flight patterns of the shots taught in the course
9. Basic rules needed to participate in a game
10. Concepts of the basic doubles systems

Psychomotor Domain

Determining definitive percentages in terms of the number of students meeting the competency standard or the degree to which the standard is met is virtually impossible because there is a degree of subjectivity in some aspects of assessment and absolute objectivity in others. However, the objectives presented here should be met by the majority of students; if not, the content and conduct of the course should be reviewed.

During class play or through psychomotor skills tests, the beginning student should score at the 85% proficiency level, as judged by the teacher, or demonstrate the correct procedures for the:

1. Forehand and backhand grips
2. Change from the forehand to the backhand grip
3. Stroking procedures with each part of the sequence in order
4. Proper footwork in moving about the court
5. Specific shots taught in class

The student also should score 70% or better on the low serve test (see Chapter 8, page 126) and 75% or better on the clear test (see Chapter 8, page 130).

Intermediate Level Course Objectives

Intermediate badminton classes give students an opportunity to reinforce previously acquired skills, to become more knowledgeable about the rules and background of the sport, to acquire other psychomotor skills, to become more consistent in stroke production, and, finally, to improve competitive technique. The structure of the intermediate class should be 50% instruction and 50% competition. However, the competitive aspects of the class should be instructive in nature rather than concentrated solely on winning. At this level, 80% of the students should be able to perform at an 80% proficiency level in each area.

Affective Domain

Intermediate students should be encouraged to analyze their own skill needs and develop appropriate practice and conditioning patterns. Behavioral objectives in the affective domain should reflect these concerns. Thus, the majority of intermediate students should:

1. Understand the value of practice in skill development, e.g., practicing voluntarily.
2. Understand the need for improving physical condition, e.g., participating voluntarily in more intense physical activity or exercise in and out of class.

3. Be able to adjust to partners, e.g., playing acceptable doubles positions and not interfering with the partner.
4. Appreciate and practice the etiquette of the sport, e.g., using the customary practices in both the instructive and the competitive phases of the class.
5. Understand the need to keep the equipment in good condition, e.g., properly storing rackets, shuttles, and nets.

Cognitive Domain

The intermediate class should demonstrate an increase in both the depth and the scope of knowledge. At the end of the course, 80% of the students should, at the 85% proficiency level, be able to diagram or write short essay answers to questions about:

1. The dimensions of all court areas
2. The development of badminton as a sport
3. The dates of the founding of the United States Badminton Association and the International Badminton Federation
4. The terms related to the sport as presented in class
5. The proper court positions for the front-back, side-by-side, and combination systems of doubles play
6. The principles of doubles play during offense and defense as discussed in class

Psychomotor Domain

Intermediate students should become proficient in additional skills as well as be able to perform each skill with greater consistency and accuracy. At the conclusion of the course, 80% of the students should be able to:

1. Serve 6 of 10 serves over the net under a string 6 inches high and into an area 1 foot square at the corner of the short line and center line.
2. Hit 7 of 10 clears from the doubles long service line into the back alley.
3. Hit 6 of 10 drop shots from the back alley into an area 2 feet deep on the opponent's side of the net.
4. Return 5 of 10 smashes into the opponent's court.
5. With his or her partner's help, keep the shuttle in play for 10 consecutive shots at the net.
6. Hit 5 of 10 backhand clears from the back alley that pass midcourt on the opponent's end.
7. Hit 5 of 10 round-the-head shots into the opponent's court.
8. Serve 7 of 10 singles serves into the back alley within 5 feet of the centerline of the appropriate service court.

Advanced Level Course Objectives

Advanced level instruction should consist of approximately 25% instruction and 75% competition. The goals of advanced instruction are consistency in stroke production, a comprehensive understanding of the badminton rules, and the ability to officiate a match. At this level, 90% of students should be able to perform at an 85% proficiency level in each of the three domains.

Affective Domain

At the advanced level, the affective domain focuses on behavior and attitudes extending beyond the class and into the tournament sphere. During and at the end of the course, the majority of advanced students should:

1. Appreciate the value of officials in a match, e.g., acknowledging the officials' presence at the conclusion of each match.
2. Understand that ill-mannered conduct has a negative effect on the game, e.g., becoming outwardly angry at calls that appear to go against themselves or their team.
3. Appreciate badminton as a sport that provides a high degree of inner satisfaction, e.g., stating a desire to participate in tournaments and to practice whenever possible.
4. Appreciate the skill of the opponent, e.g., recognizing and even acknowledging an opponent's good shots.
5. Appreciate the value of helping other players.
6. Understand the need to keep the equipment in good condition, e.g., properly storing rackets, shuttles, and nets.

Cognitive Domain

Advanced students should be familiar with the more minute details of the sport. By the end of the course, they should be able to:

1. Show knowledge of the rules of badminton, e.g., achieving a 90% score on a comprehensive written test.
2. Demonstrate officiating ability, e.g., umpiring an intramural tournament or a class contest.
3. Analyze another player's skill, e.g., completing a checklist of their partner's stroke performance and comparing it to a similar list prepared by the instructor.
4. Describe the mechanics of all shots in a written examination.
5. Outline the procedures for organizing a badminton tournament.

Psychomotor Domain

At the advanced level, the psychomotor domain is concerned with the consistency of stroke production, the ability to perform all strokes, and the tactical aspects of the game. At the conclusion of the course, 90% of advanced students should be able to:

1. Perform all shots learned in class with 85% or better proficiency.
2. Demonstrate any of the three systems of doubles play during competition.
3. Demonstrate knowledge of the basic principles of strategy during play, e.g., moving to a front-back position when on attack and to a side-by-side position when on the defensive.

SUGGESTED PROJECTS

The following projects may be of help to the beginning teacher and/or students in preparation programs:

1. Talk to an experienced instructor. After determining his or her objectives for a specific class, write them in behavioral terms.

2. Review this chapter's affective domain objectives for the beginning, intermediate, and advanced levels. Prepare a checklist for one or two of the objectives in one level and then observe a badminton class. Does your checklist enable you to evaluate student performance?

3

Equipment and Facilities

Most school and agency facilities are constructed to serve generalized rather than specialized instructional programs; therefore, consideration must be given to providing badminton teachers and students with a better instructional environment. Physical education equipment must be of sufficient quality to enhance the learning experiences of students. Rackets that are too heavy or too loosely strung and thus make students overexert themselves to produce a shot, shuttles that come apart, or nets of such small mesh that the entire flight of the shuttle cannot be followed cannot provide experiences that encourage further participation in the sport. However, equipment that gives students positive results with average effort soon provides them with a sense of success. The equipment listed below should provide students with a measure of success soon after instruction begins. Because manufacturers often change models, prices and quality should be checked when new purchases are made to be sure that similar value for the same price is obtained.

PURCHASE OF EQUIPMENT

The purchase of physical education equipment should be based on the advice of instructors, who usually are more knowledgeable about such equipment than administrative personnel. Too often consideration is given only to the lowest price, disregarding overall economy. The quality of physical education equipment must be such that it can withstand hard daily use and provide students with a realistic experience and a reasonable measure of success.

All badminton instructors are encouraged to become acquainted with manufacturers and suppliers who specialize in badminton equipment because they (1) are usually more interested in promoting the sport than in just selling equipment, (2) can help the school or agency by recommending equipment that matches its financial means, and (3) can answer various technical questions. When purchase of equipment is beyond a school's means, a teacher desiring to include badminton in the instructional program has several options: (1) Students who have rackets can be asked to bring them to class. (2) The community can be surveyed to see whether people who have equipment would be willing to

The portions of this chapter related to rackets, shuttles, and nets appear through the courtesy of Charles Norton, President, Louisville Badminton Supply, 9411 Westport Road, Louisville, Kentucky 40222. All prices and descriptions are from the *Catalog of the Louisville Badminton Supply, 1981*. Used and quoted with permission.

donate it to the school. (3) the Parent-Teacher Association (PTA) might be encouraged to purchase badminton equipment as a project. If some of the necessary equipment could be obtained from these sources, the school may be able to find ways to purchase the balance.

Nets

Although the rules of badminton specify the official dimensions for a net, many nets sold today do not meet these specifications. The size of the net is only one of many factors to consider when purchasing nets.

On today's market, the price of a net ranges from approximately $6 to $26. Since nets last for some time given the proper care, it is best to buy a grade of net that meets official specifications. An underlying assumption here is that all students will be instructed in the proper care of all equipment and that these regulations will be posted, distributed, or explained in class and will be strictly enforced.

Since most gymnasiums cannot afford the luxury of singles *and* doubles courts, lines are usually put down for doubles play. Thus, nets should always be a minimum of 20 feet and a maximum of 21 feet in length. When more than one court is to be used, all nets should be strung on a single nylon cord. A loop should be made in each of the lines and a spring attached. Then the other end of the spring can be attached either to the eyelet at the 5-foot 1-inch level on a standard fastened to the floor (Figure 3.1) or to an eyebolt fastened flush to the wall, the center of which is 5 feet 1 inch from the floor.

Wooden standards (Figure 3.2) can be constructed at school (Appendix A) and placed on the sidelines of each court at the net, thereby making it easy to keep the net at the official height of 5 feet 1 inch at the posts and 5 feet at the center. Nets prepared in this way should be used whenever the

Figure 3.1
Spring attached to eyebolt

Figure 3.2
Wooden standards

Figure 3.3
Folding the net

entire facility is to be set up. When only one court is to be used, procedures for setting up one net should be developed. Clearly they will vary according to the facility.

Students must be shown the proper way to put up and take down badminton nets. The simplest way to dismantle a net is to disconnect the net cord from the spring at one end of the floor. Then the net is folded back and forth upon itself at arm's length until it is completely folded (Figure 3.3). The attached end provides enough tension to make folding the net easy. The springs are removed from the eyelets or eyebolts and placed with the nets, which have been folded in half, and the standards are removed. Finally, everything is stored. Table 3.1 lists several recommended nets.

Rackets

Badminton rackets currently range in price from approximately $6 to $60. They are manufactured from many different materials and combinations of materials. Rackets purchased for class use should have the following characteristics:

1. The racket should weigh about 5 ounces. It should be firmly strung with nylon; gut string is too expensive and steel strings are not resilient enough.
2. The racket should have a five-ply laminated head of beech or ash, without fiber inserts, and a metal shaft. This type of racket retains its shape better than all-metal rackets.
3. The racket should be evenly balanced and curve evenly when bent. This can be tested by holding the end of the head and the handle with the thumb of each hand toward the center of the

Table 3.1
Recommended Nets

Manufacture	Model	Headbands	Mesh	Depth	Length	Price (approx.)	Description
Coast Marketing Group*		3 in.	¾ in.	2½ ft	21 ft	$21	Meets official specifications; bound on all sides; vinyl headband makes folding more difficult
Victory*	4506	3 in.	¾ in.	2½ ft	21 ft	$18	Meets official specifications; bound on all sides; canvas headband facilitates folding
Victory†	4504	Canvas	NA	NA	NA	$15	NA
Sportcraft†	00434	1¼ in.	1¼ in.	2½ ft	21 ft	$13	NA

NA = not available
*Strongly recommended
†Recommended if price is a factor

Figure 3.4
Testing racket

shaft. The hands press down while the thumbs exert upward pressure causing the racket to bend (Figure 3.4). When the pressure is released, the racket should return to its normal shape.
4. Grip sizes range from 3⅜ to 3⅝ inches. Less expensive rackets have a standard grip size of 3½ inches. Others are available in graduated sizes. The racket grip must be in proportion to the size of the player's hand. Table 3.2 presents a suggested ratio of grip sizes for different age groups. Grips should be covered with leather for better control of the racket and should be rectangular in shape (Figure 3.5). The rectangular shape is better suited to the hand than a square one.
5. When not in use, rackets should be kept in a press, hung in a rack, or hung from a hook to keep them from warping.

Table 3.2
Suggested Ratio of Grip Sizes

	Grip Size 3⅜ in.	Grip Size 3½ in.	Grip Size 3⅝ in.
Junior high students	80%	10%	10%
Senior high students	75%	15%	10%
Adults	20%	75%	10%

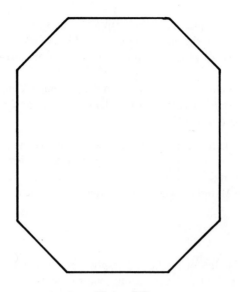

Figure 3.5
End view of racket handle showing its rectangular shape

Since rackets for class use are generally purchased by the school or agency, Table 3.3 serves as a buying guide for beginning teachers.

There are all-steel rackets with steel strings sold on the market. Because of their weight, grip size, lack of string resiliency, detrimental effect on shuttles, difficulty of repair, and cost, these rackets are not recommended.

Advanced, intermediate, and experienced beginning players may want to purchase their own rackets. They should be advised as follows:

1. A frame should be purchased and then be strung. The choice of nylon or gut depends on the player's performance, but in either case the frame should be of good quality. Good frames alone

Table 3.3
Recommended Rackets

Manufacturer	Model	Ply	Grip Material/Size	String	Price (approx.)
Dunhill*	NA	6	Leather/Standard	Nylon	$10
Sportcraft*	Stamina	5	Leather/NA	Nylon	$16
Yonex†	B9100	5	Leather/Assorted	Nylon	$37

NA = not available

*Recommended for beginning classes

†Recommended for intermediate and advanced classes

begin at about $18 with string prices ranging from $2.10 to $4 for nylon and $10 to $14 for gut.

2. The grip size depends on how the player prefers to hold the racket, in the fingers or in the hand. The trend seems to be toward smaller-sized (3⅜-inch) grips because they are more easily held in the fingers.

3. The balance point can be closer to the head or to the grip depending on whether a light or heavy head is desired. For an evenly balanced racket, the balance point should be midway between the top of the head and the end of the handle.

To keep rackets in good condition, instructional staff members should be taught how to restring them. When wood rackets are strung, the holes through which the string passes must be smooth; for metal or composition rackets, nylon grommets or other material must be used to keep the string from being frayed by sharp edges. Materials needed to restring rackets include awls, tension gauges, string, and a racket vise.

Shuttlecocks

Shuttlecocks are made of nylon or feathers. The price of a dozen nylon shuttles ranges from approximately $8.10 to $12, and of a dozen feather shuttlecocks from $14 to $17. Today's nylon shuttlecocks have flight characteristics similar to those of feather shuttles. However, they are more durable than feather shuttles and thus more economical and practical.

Shuttlecocks weigh 73 to 85 grains (average 77-79 grains) and are manufactured for different speeds, for play on courts with low or poor visibility, for high altitudes, and for outdoor play. Outdoor shuttles are heavier and have a larger base than indoor shuttles; they are also marked as outdoor shuttles. Most badminton associations and organizations have approved nylon shuttles for tournament play. Table 3.4 lists recommended indoor shuttles, all approved by the United States Badminton Association.

Table 3.4
Recommended Indoor Shuttles

Manufacturer	Model	Speed	Price (approx. per dozen)	Description
Carlton	Tournament Blue 00201	Medium	$11	A good nylon shuttle for class use; fluted skirt simulates flight of a feathered shuttle
Carlton	International Blue 00289	Medium	$10	Similar to preceding shuttle; skirt is not quite as stiff
Carlton	Tournament Plus 00292	Medium	$14	Similar to preceding shuttles but has a stiffer skirt
H L	Trueflite	NA	$10	Skirt is made of Zytel^{TM}, cork base with kid; a good shuttle with excellent flight characteristics

NA = not available

A minimum of one shuttle for each student should be available; however, the recommended ratio is three shuttles per student. This ratio enables the student to practice or perform specific duties without having to retrieve shuttles quite so often.

CARE OF EQUIPMENT

Students must be taught that the nets, rackets, and shuttlecocks will serve them well as long as they exercise care in their use. The following points should be emphasized:

1. To prevent a racket from slipping out of the hands, the player's hands and racket grip should be dried regularly.
2. Rackets should not be swung or thrown at the net, standards, or wall or hit on the floor in anger.
3. To avoid the clashing of rackets during doubles play, shuttles hit between two players, i.e., down the middle, should be taken by the forehand player. When a right-handed player and left-handed player are playing together, the one with the better backhand should take those shots.
4. In doubles, partners should learn to communicate with each other to avoid collisions and clashing of rackets.
5. Shuttlecocks should be held by the base so that the skirt is not bent out of shape, thus making good flight patterns impossible.
6. During play or practice, extra shuttles should be placed near the standards. They should be stored separately from the rackets in containers, with their base down.
7. Older shuttles should be used before and after class until the true flight pattern cannot be maintained. Then they should be discarded.
8. Rackets should be checked daily for broken strings, cracked frames, and loose grips. Repairs should be made immediately so that the equipment is always in playable condition.

PRACTICE AREA

Figure 3.6 illustrates how a gymnasium can be made more useful for badminton play. Two parallel lines can be painted on the wall (A) of the gymnasium for use in low serve practice. The top of the bottom line (B) should be 5 feet from the floor, and the bottom of the top line (C) should be 6 inches above the lower line. A series of 1-foot lines (D) should be painted 3 feet apart on the floor (E) 8½ feet from the wall. These lines should be painted parallel to the wall.

Adequate lighting is a must. Burned-out bulbs should be replaced immediately. Floors should be kept free of dust and any other debris that might cause a player to fall.

Facilities should be set up and the equipment readied prior to the start of class if at all possible to give students some practice time. Similarly, practice after class should be encouraged, with the instructor always being on hand to help students. Careful preparation and use of the facilities and equipment ensure the development of good badminton skills.

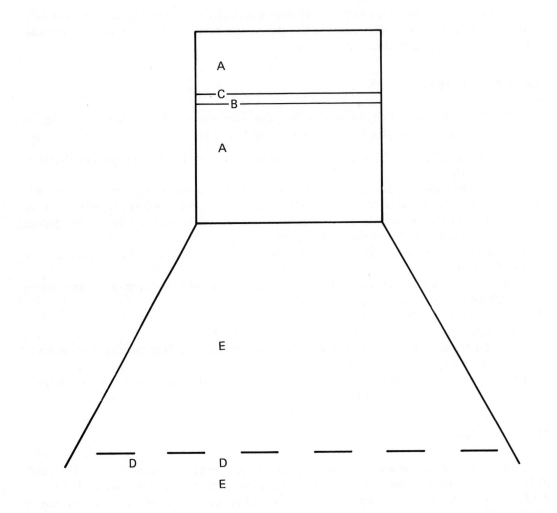

Figure 3.6
Preparation of gymnasium wall and floor for low service practice

4

Class Organization

Teaching badminton involves more than passing out the equipment and letting students play. Consideration must be given to the appropriate procedures for conducting a class; otherwise the course objectives will not be met. This chapter covers the first class meeting, formations for use in class, the development and use of demonstrations, aids for practicing strokes, and the distribution and collection of equipment.

FIRST CLASS MEETING

The most important consideration in teaching is the ability of the teacher and the student to communicate, to understand one another's expectations. Therefore, the first meeting of the group or class is the most important because it sets the tone.

During the first meeting, the instructor should have available (1) any relevant handout material, (2) course requirements, (3) course objectives, (4) operating procedures for the course, and (5) evaluation procedures. The game of badminton could be introduced via a game film or an exhibition game by local players if available. The ideal situation would be to bring all students enrolled in badminton classes together for this introductory meeting so that everyone learns simultaneously what the course requires. Following this meeting, students attend their laboratory classes to learn the skills involved in badminton. Final written examinations could also be handled in the large group.

CLASS FORMATIONS

The instructor's choice of formations depends on the size of the class. When the instructor uses a chalkboard, students should be seated in a semicircle in front of the board so that all can see it clearly. When the instructor plans to put diagrams on the board, he or she should do so, whenever possible, before the start of class.

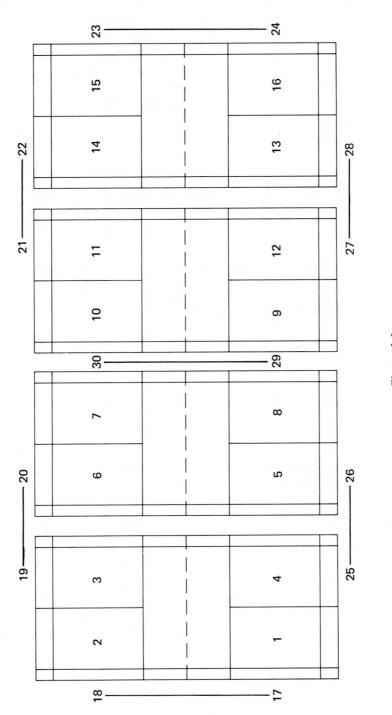

Figure 4.1
Facility arrangement for class of 30 students

Small groups—the number of students equal to or less than the number of courts times four—enable the instructor to work almost exclusively on the courts. When there is one less than a full complement of students, the instructor has one-half of a court available for working with students who need individual help. For example, the instructor, who can place the shuttle at a specific point, can use this court to assist a student with his or her stroke development.

Although four students to a court is the basic recommendation for class size, administrative demands sometimes do not permit this. When there are more students than the courts can hold, the courts, the space between the courts, and the walls must be used. Although court arrangement varies with each particular procedure, Figure 4.1 shows one general arrangement for a class of 30 students. This arrangement can be used when students are hitting together because court lines are not important. (The numbers 1, 2, 19, 28, etc., represent students and their placement.)

For the teaching of the low service, certain court lines are significant. Students can be arranged on each court as shown in Figure 4.2 (Again, the numbers represent students.) For hairpin net flights, a minimum amount of space is needed. Figure 4.3 shows an arrangement for the teaching of this skill. In footwork drills, students can be arranged in the center of each court (Figure 4.4). This formation can be used only when the drill does not include stroking the shuttle.

At times a particular drill limits the number of students to two or four per court. In those instances, the perimeters of the court can be used. Some students can be assigned the low service practice area, while others can use the wall for overhead and underhand stroke practice. (Techniques for using the wall are discussed in Chapter 6.) Although smooth walls are preferred, cement block walls can be used even though the recessed seams at times affect the rebound of the shuttle.) Figure 4.5 illustrates a possible arrangement for this situation.

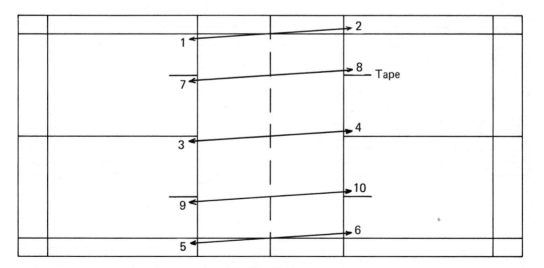

Figure 4.2
Students arranged on court for low service practice

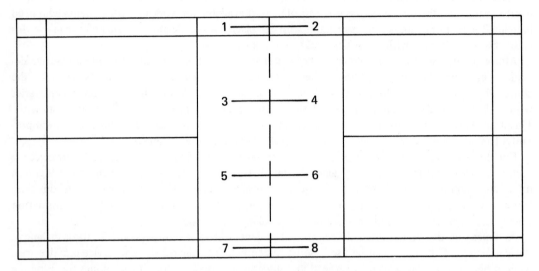

Figure 4.3
Students arranged on court for hairpin net flight practice

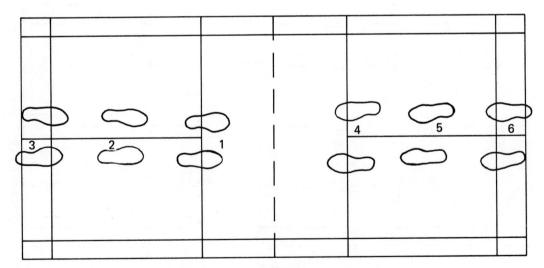

Figure 4.4
Students arranged on court for side-to-side footwork drills

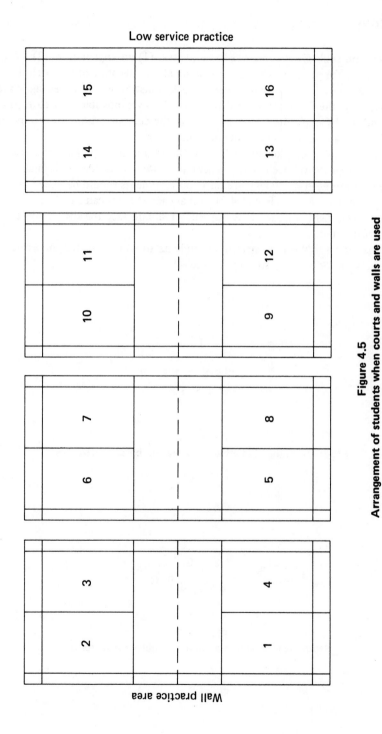

Figure 4.5
Arrangement of students when courts and walls are used

DEMONSTRATIONS

Teaching badminton skills always involves three phases: (1) an explanation, (2) a demonstration, and (3) an opportunity for practice. The demonstration allows the student to watch the performance of the skill to be learned. Like all audiovisual aids, demonstrations emphasizing a specific point should be prepared by the instructor ahead of time whenever possible. Moreover, the instructor should prepare students by explaining the main point of the demonstration prior to the presentation. Then he or she should evaluate the value of the demonstration.

The demonstration can be conducted by the instructor, a skilled student, or a visiting player. It should be the second phase of each new element presented or reviewed throughout the course.

When a demonstration need not take place on a court, students should be seated in a block formation (Figure 4.6) or in a semicircle (Figure 4.7) so that each student can clearly see the instructor. If a window or any strong light is a factor, the instructor should face the distraction so that the students' vision is unobstructed.

When a court is used for the demonstration, students should be seated alongside the court at the end where the instructor is demonstrating (Figure 4.8).

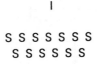

Figure 4.6
Students arranged in a block formation before instructor

Figure 4.7
Students arranged in a semicircle before instructor

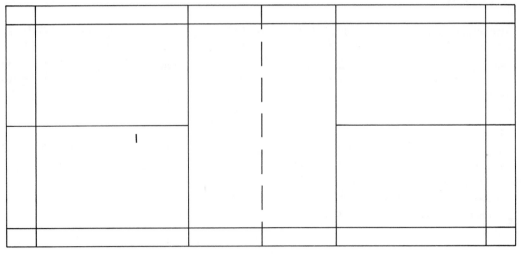

x x x x x x x x x x x x
x x x x x x x x x x x

Figure 4.8
Students arranged in a block formation alongside court to watch demonstration

Figure 4.9
Fleece balls arranged at various heights

STROKE PRACTICE

Stroke practice can be enhanced by stretching a wire, line, or chain approximately 12 feet high across the gymnasium and hanging fleece balls (Figure 4.9) or shuttles from it with fishing line or string. For the most satisfactory results, the objects to be hit should hang at various heights so there is one appropriate for each student. The appropriate height of this object can be determined by the following procedures:

1. Mark on a wall in 1-inch increments a vertical distance of 3 feet beginning at the height of 78 inches.
2. Have each student stand at the mark and extend the racket straight up over his or her head (Figure 4.10).
3. Check and record the height at the center of the racket.
4. Select the appropriate object and attach it to the wire.
5. Assign each student to the appropriate station for stroke practice.

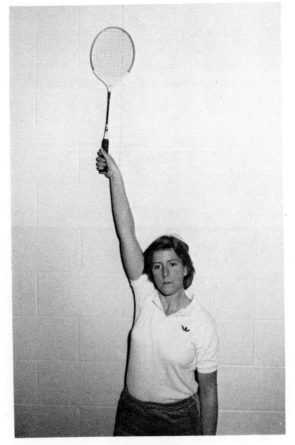

Figure 4.10

The wire, line, or chain can be wrapped with tape to prevent the object from sliding more than an inch or so. When struck with a flat racket, the object then spins straight around the wire. When struck obliquely, the object then slides in the direction the racket head faces.

EQUIPMENT DISTRIBUTION AND COLLECTION

The instructor must also explain to the class or group the procedure for obtaining rackets and shuttles for class use, e.g., either the instructor brings the equipment to the gymnasium in a case or rack or each student is issued a racket and shuttle from the equipment room. When possible, the instructor should have the equipment available for use before and after class, thus giving students as much practice time as possible.

STUDENT PROJECT

Using a diagram of any gymnasium with three badminton courts, prepare a chart outlining possible court arrangements for classes of 16, 22, 30, and 44 students.

5 Teaching Beginning Badminton

Optimally, a beginning badminton class consists of 20 to 30 lessons, each involving 35 to 40 minutes of instruction. This chapter presents an outline of each individual lesson that includes these aspects: (1) preparation, (2) content and concepts, and (3) teaching aids and techniques.

Instruction for beginning students is designed to provide them with knowledge and understanding of the basic playing skills and the ability to execute them well. Playing of the game during class is designed to give students an opportunity to practice skills in a meaningful situation; winning each game is not the ultimate goal at this level.

LESSON 1: ORIENTATION

I. Preparation

Have handouts ready. These may include a student outline for the class, course regulations, a glossary of badminton terms, background information, and a summary of the badminton rules.

II. Content and Concepts

A. Ascertain students' playing experience and any medical restrictions.

B. Discuss the appropriate attire for class, the care of equipment, and student evaluation procedures.

C. Discuss the background, international status, and advantages of badminton. Table 5.1 provides a summary of all this material.

D. When possible, permit students to practice hitting. This effective motivational technique allows the instructor to evaluate the overall skill of the class at an early stage. If hitting is done, step C may have to be covered in Lesson 2.

Table 5.1
Information to Be Presented in First Class

Appropriate Attire

When the school issues clothes or requires a specific uniform, students must use it

If a uniform is not needed, clothing must be loose enough to permit freedom of movement but not so loose that it interferes with stroking

Shoes must fit well and be lightweight and cushioned

Wearing one or two pair of socks can help protect player's feet; this is somewhat a matter of individual preference

Care of Equipment

Courts are set up and equipment made available before class starts

Procedure for obtaining and returning racket and shuttlecock varies with situation

Racket grip and hands should be wiped periodically to prevent racket from slipping out of one's grasp

Shuttles should be picked up by hand at base or by heavier ribs; extra shuttles should be kept in containers or placed by standards, making damage during practice or play less likely

If a racket is broken, tell instructor immediately; if it is broken because of carelessness or anger, the offending student must pay for its repair or replacement

At end of day, rackets and shuttlecocks should be inspected and broken rackets and worn shuttles replaced

Student Evaluation

Varies with the situation

Should be related to course objectives

Should include tests of performance skills:
a. Basic stroking procedure
b. Ability to perform basic strokes
c. Low service test
d. Clear test

Should include tests on:
a. Badminton rules
b. Etiquette
c. Terms
d. Other pertinent information

Background

May be composite of older games (e.g., poona and battledore and shuttlecock)

Named after the estate (Badminton) of the Duke of Beaufort; first game probably played in the Great Hall about 1870 to 1873

Introduced in United States by Bayard Clark and E. Landon Wilkes in 1878

Did not become popular in United States until after 1920

In many countries (e.g., Malaya, Japan, Indonesia, England, Denmark), ranks as a national sport

International Status

Earliest association was the Badminton Association of England organized 1893

The United States Badminton Association (formerly named American Badminton Association), governing body for badminton in U.S., was founded in 1936

The Thomas Cup (men) and Uber Cup (women) are symbolic of the world team championships; these competitions are held every 3 years

Present holder of the Thomas Cup is _____
_____

Present holder of the Uber Cup is _____
_____

Advantages of the Game

Is easy to learn to play reasonably well—gives satisfaction early

Is ideal sport for everyone

Can be played at different levels of ability

Is a fine recreational game for all because sets are inexpensive

Acceleration and deceleration properties of shuttle make game potentially quite slow or very fast

Involves as much or more physical exertion as baseball or football at similar levels of competition

Depends more on agility and deception than strength and speed

Complements tennis and other racket sports

LESSON 2: RACKET NOMENCLATURE AND THE GRIP

I. Preparation

A. Bring handouts.
B. Check any medical restrictions of new students.

II. Content and Concepts

A. Physical Conditioning. This important aspect of any physical education class should be a part of all sessions. Exercises should be general in nature and promote arm and shoulder strength (push-ups and pull-ups), abdominal strength (sit-ups), endurance (shuttle runs, distance runs), and flexibility (stretching).

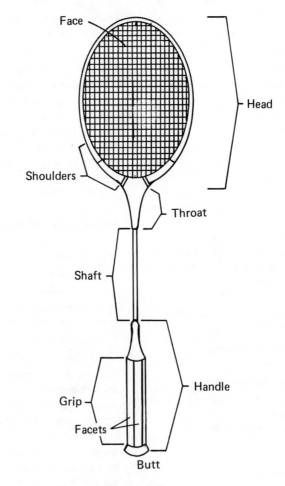

Figure 5.1
Racket nomenclature

B. Racket Nomenclature. Before a student can learn badminton, she or he must become familiar with the parts of the racket (Figure 5.1). As each student holds a racket, identify its:

1. Head—oval part of the top of the racket
2. Face—hitting surface
3. Shoulders—curved, reinforced section connecting the throat to the head
4. Throat—junction of the head with the shaft
5. Shaft—long, slender section running into the handle
6. Handle—the lower, thicker hexagonal part of racket into which the shaft is set
7. Grip—leather-covered portion of the handle
8. Facets—eight flat, angled sections making up the grip
9. Butt—built-up end of the grip

C. The Grip. This connects the player, racket, and shuttle. The correct grip facilitates the
striking of the shuttle on the forehand or backhand. The mobility of the hand at the wrist
is a significant factor in the generation of racket head speed and deception.

1. A method of assuming the forehand grip is shown in Figure 5.2A through E.
2. An alternative method of assuming the forehand grip is presented in Figure 5.3A,
   B, and C.

**Figure 5.2A through E
Procedures for assuming the forehand grip**

**Figure 5.2A
Hold racket in front of body in off-racket hand**

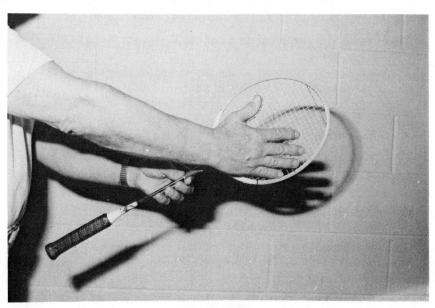

Figure 5.2B
Place palm of racket-side hand on racket face

Figure 5.2C
Slide racket-side hand down racket shaft until heel of the hand touches butt plate of racket

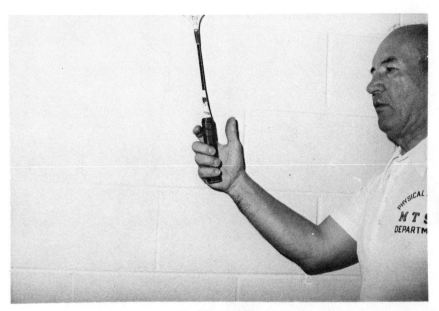

Figure 5.2D
Wrap slightly spread fingers diagonally around racket grip

Figure 5.2E
Wrap thumb diagonally around racket grip, with thumb contacting middle finger at the first joint

Figure 5.3A through C
Alternate procedures for assuming the forehand grip

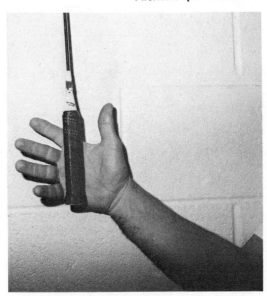

Figure 5.3A
Hold racket-side hand flat with palm up;
place racket on the hand as shown

Figure 5.3B
Wrap slightly spread fingers diagonally
around racket handle

Figure 5.3C
Wrap thumb around racket grip diagonally with thumb contacting middle finger at first joint

·3. Checkpoints for the grip are as follows:

    a. The "V" of the thumb and forefinger should be located on the top facet of the racket.

    b. Generally, four knuckles should be visible when a player holds the racket in front of himself or herself. However, only three knuckles will show if a student has a smaller-than-average hand.

    c. The racket should be an extension of the player's arm and in line with rather than perpendicular to it.

    d. The racket must be held firmly but not tightly in the fingers. The fingers tighten on racket prior to impact with shuttle.

    e. Grip should not inhibit wrist action.

4. Figure 5.4 shows where the points of pressure are located when the racket is being held correctly.

5. The procedures for teaching the forehand grip are as follows:

    a. Arrange students in a semi-circle around yourself.

    b. Explain and demonstrate how the forehand grip is assumed.

    c. Have students practice assuming the grip.

    d. Check each student's grip and make corrections as needed.

    e. Stress that patience and vigilance are needed to master the forehand grip.

    f. Stress that the forehand grip is to be used when hitting all shuttles on the forehand side of the body.*

*To avoid the terms "left" and "right" the terms "forehand" and "backhand" are used, respectively. Forehand refers to a stroke used when the shuttle is on the *racket side* of the midline of the body. Backhand refers to a stroke used when the shuttle is on the *off-racket side* of the midline of the body.

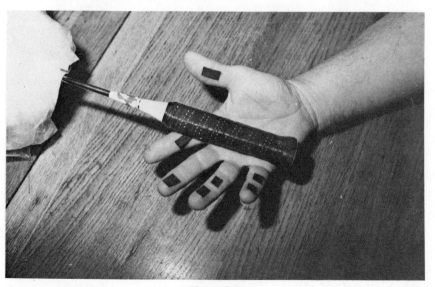

Figure 5.4.
Pressure points

6. The procedures for changing the forehand grip to the backhand grip are as follows:

   a. Holding the racket in a forehand grip, allow top edge of racket to turn one-eighth turn away from the midline of the body (Figure 5.5A and B).

   b. Bring the index finger down toward the middle finger.

   c. Extend the thumb along the back facet of the handle for increased leverage; this is known as the "thumb up" backhand.

   d. The "V" of the thumb and forefinger is aligned on the inside top facet of the grip.

7. The procedures for teaching the backhand grip are as follows:

   a. Arrange students in semicircle around yourself.

   b. Explain and demonstrate how to change from the forehand grip to the backhand grip.

   c. Have students practice changing the grip.

   d. Check each student's grip and make corrections as needed.

   e. Stress that this grip is to be used when hitting all shuttles on backhand side of body; the only exception is the round-the-head shot.

Figure 5.5A and B
Change of racket position from forehand to backhand grip

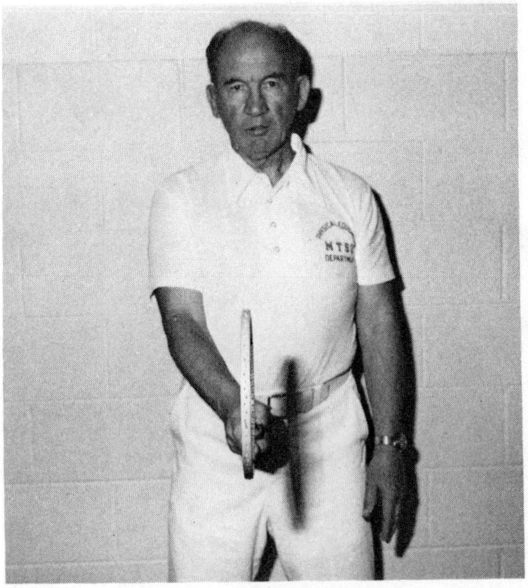

Figure 5.5A
Forehand

Figure 5.5B
Backhand

D. Wrist Action. Although there is some discussion about the importance of the "wrist snap," the need to cock the wrist prior to hitting all shots proves there is some movement of the hand at the wrist. For any action at the wrist to be functional, the racket must be loosely held. The instructor should demonstrate this action and then have students:

1. Grip the racket as tightly as possible.
2. Attempt to move the racket back and forth easily.
3. Note the difficulty of making this movement.
4. Loosen their grip.
5. Again attempt to move the racket back and forth.
6. Note the subsequent ease of making this movement.

E. Hand-Eye Coordination Drill. The key to success in badminton is the ability to hit the shuttle with the racket in a controlled manner. This action involves perception, timing, and correct movement of the racket. A simple but effective hand-eye coordination drill gives the student an opportunity to practice these skills individually by hitting shuttles into the air in consecutive fashion. Proficiency is achieved when the student can hit 10 to 15 consecutive shuttles without moving more than two or three steps.

1. The procedures for executing this drill are:

    a. Find a place on the floor where there is room to swing the racket freely.
    b. Hold the shuttle at the base between the thumb and forefinger.
    c. Hold the racket back about waist high, with the wrist cocked.
    d. Drop the shuttle, then swing the racket with an underhand stroke at the shuttle.
    e. Just prior to contact, snap the racket head through the shot by flexing the hand at the wrist and pronating and inwardly rotating the arm.
    f. Make contact with the shuttle holding the arm relatively straight and the racket head parallel with the floor.
    g. After achieving reasonable control with the forehand, attempt the same drill with the backhand.
    h. Alternate forehand and backhand strokes, being sure to modify the grip each time.

2. After a demonstration by the instructor, students should practice hitting the shuttle with control and appropriate arm and wrist action. As the students practice the drill, the instructor should circulate and correct errors. Errors and corrections related to the hand-eye coordination drill are listed in Table 5.2.

III. Teaching Techniques and Aids

A. The proper "feel" of a particular grip is more easily obtained when a template that demonstrates the correct grip is developed and made available to students. Templates for left-handed and right-handed students must be prepared.
B. The procedure for preparing a template is as follows:

1. Spread a light coating of powder over the racket grip.
2. Dampen the hand *very* slightly and grasp the racket with the correct forehand or backhand grip.
3. Remove the hand and cover the clear leather with pieces of ¼-inch or ½-inch tape.

C. Figure 5.6 shows two prepared grips.

Table 5.2
Errors and Corrections for Hand-Eye Coordination Drill

Error	Correction
Shuttle flies off at a tangent	Position the racket head parallel to floor on contact with shuttle and the shuttle perpendicular to racket head
Arm action is from the elbow	Emphasize that the axis of rotation is from the shoulder; arm should be straight
Follow-through is with flexion of hand at the wrist	Keep arm straight; pronate and inwardly rotate it on the forehand; supinate and outwardly rotate it on the backhand
Hitting is done with same hitting surface on both sides	Change grip so that the palm of the hand is leading stroke when shuttle is on the forehand side and the back of the hand is leading when shuttle is on the backhand side
Same foot is put forward for hitting all shots	Be sure that the off-racket foot is forward on the forehand and that the racket-side foot is forward on the backhand

Figure 5.6
Prepared grips

LESSON 3: STANCE AND STROKING

I. Preparation

    A. Bring handouts.

    B. Check any medical restrictions of new students.

    C. Have the courts set up for use by early arrivals.

II. Content and Concepts

    A. Physical Conditioning. Exercises can be led by the instructor or a student leader.

    B. Review and Warm-up. Students practice grips and the hand-eye coordination drill while the instructor circulates and makes corrections as needed. All corrections should be positive in nature, i.e., tell students what *should be done* rather than what should not be done.

    C. Stance and Stroking. Sound preparation, the basis of good stroke production, begins with the ready position (Table 5.3 and Figure 5.7). From the ready position, the player executes

Table 5.3
Establishing a Ready Position and Executing Forehand and Backhand Shots

Establishing Ready Position	Executing Forehand Shots (cont)
Spread feet about a shoulders' width apart	As shoulders rotate inward, arm begins to straighten
Place off-racket foot slightly ahead of racket-side foot	When arm is straight, cocked wrist has racket perpendicular to arm or parallel to floor
Evenly distribute weight on balls of both feet	Uncock wrist and turn thumb toward body
Slightly bend knees	Racket head is perpendicular to flight of shuttle on contact
Incline upper body forward from waist	Following contact, racket follows through naturally, ending below hand
Keep head up, with eyes alert and focused on shuttle	Return to ready position
Hold racket out in front of body, approximately head high	**Executing Backhand Shots**
Cock wrist	Change grip from forehand to backhand
Executing Forehand Shots	Pivot on ball of off-racket side foot
Pivot on ball of racket-side foot	Point racket-side of body toward net
Bring racket straight back to position behind head, extending down back	Complete backswing as pivot is completed
Point off-racket shoulder toward net	At completion of backswing, racket head is at off-racket shoulder, elbow is bent, palm of hand is face down
Align elbow of racket-side arm with shoulders	Point elbow at shuttle—*up* for overheads, *down* for low shots, *toward net* for drives
Cock wrist	Racket continues through arc as thumb of racket hand turns outward to put hitting surface of racket in hitting position
Place weight on rear foot	Shuttle must be in front of body
Focus eyes on shuttle	
Step forward with off-racket foot	
Transfer weight from rear foot to front foot	
Rotate hips toward midline of body as momentum begins to build	

*Kenneth R. Davidson and Lealand R. Gustavson, *Winning Badminton* (New York: A. S. Barnes and Company, 1953), p. 17.

Figure 5.7
Ready position

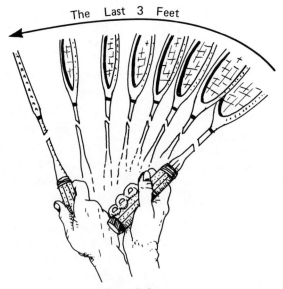

Figure 5.8
The hitting range

After Kenneth R. Davidson and Leland R. Gustavson, published by A. S. Barnes & Company, Inc., 1953. All rights reserved. By permission of the publisher.

forehand and backhand strokes. The hitting range* is the last 1 meter (3 feet) of the racket's motion prior to contact with the shuttle. Hitting power, speed, control, and deception are determined within this range (Figure 5.8). When the player is stroking, the wrist must be cocked for all shots and the arm inwardly rotated in order to place the racket head in a perpendicular position (flat) to the shuttle at contact. The speed of these movements and the resultant force vary with the type of stroke. Table 5.3 also describes the execution of the forehand and backhand strokes.

D. Procedures for Teaching the Ready Position and Forehand and Backhand Strokes. Figure 5.9 shows the ready position; Figure 5.10 A through D, the forehand stroke; and Figure 5.11 A through D, the backhand stroke.

1. Arrange students in two parallel lines facing you.
2. Explain and demonstrate the ready position, emphasizing the points listed in Table 5.3.
3. Then ask students to spread out and assume the ready position.
4. Circulate and make corrections as needed.
5. After they have practiced the ready position, again arrange students in two parallel lines facing you.
6. Explain and demonstrate the forehand and backhand strokes.
7. Then ask students to spread out on the court.
8. Call "Ready, stroke" to have students assume ready position and execute a forehand stroke and then a backhand stroke.

Figure 5.9
Ready position

Figure 5.10A through D
Sequence for executing forehand stroke

Figure 5.10A
Place racket behind head, extending
down back

Figure 5.10B
Step forward on off-racket foot and begin
to straighten arm

Figure 5.10C
When arm is straight, racket head is perpendicular to flight of shuttle on contact

Figure 5.10D
After contact, follow through with racket

**Figure 5.11A through D
Sequence for executing backhand stroke**

Figure 5.11A
Pivot on ball of off-racket side foot and point
racket side of body toward net

Figure 5.11B
Bend elbow, with palm of hand face down;
racket head is at off-racket shoulder, elbow
pointed toward shuttle

Figure 5.11C
Contact shuttle at full extension

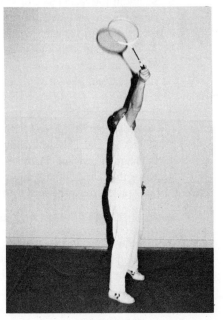

Figure 5.11D
Racket continues through arc

9. Circulate and make corrections as needed.
10. Permit students to continue stroking on their own and give individual help as necessary.

III. Teaching Techniques and Aids

A. Students must learn that the racket must continue through the arc after contact with the shuttle. The clock is a good aid for teaching this concept:

1. Visualize a clock parallel to the flight of the shuttle. The center of the clock is at the point of the shoulder. As the racket is swung, the head of the racket inscribes an arc identical to the rim of the clock (12:00 is directly overhead; 3:00 in front of the shoulder; 9:00 in back). The arm must remain in extension throughout the shot.
2. Let the clock face serve as an example. The arc inscribed by the racket follows a 180-degree arc, from 9:00 to 12:00 to 3:00. Contact with the shuttle is made at 12:00, with the racket head following through to 3:00 (Figure 5.12A, B, and C).

B. Some students learn better when manually helped through a movement pattern. This technique is most helpful for teaching the basic stroke patterns. Procedures for use of this technique are as follows:

1. Forehand (Figure 5.13A through E)

   a. Ask the student to assume the basic stroke stance with the off-racket foot forward, off-racket shoulder pointing toward the net, the racket behind the head (Figure 5.13A).
   b. Stand on the racket side of the student and grasp the hand holding the racket.
   c. Have the student step forward with the off-racket foot (Figure 5.13B) and begin to rotate the hips forward, which also moves the shoulders forward.
   d. As the student's shoulders come forward, begin to extend the student's arm so that when the shoulders are parallel to the net the arm is fully extended. The racket is still back, and the wrist is cocked in preparation for completion of the stroke (Figure 5.13C).
   e. Begin to move the player's racket through the hitting range. *The student must watch the movement of his or her arm and hand at this time.*
   f. Move the student's arm through the hitting range, calling attention to the position of the hand at contact (Figure 5.13D).
   g. Move the player's hand and racket through the follow-through and then ask the student to return to the ready position (Figure 5.13E).

2. Backhand (Figures 5.14A through E)

   a. Ask the student to assume the basic backhand stroke stance.
   b. Stand at the side and to the rear of the player's racket side (Figure 5.14A).
   c. Hold the student's hand and have the student step forward as weight shifts forward (Figure 5.14B).
   d. As this is done, move player's arm through the stroke (Figure 5.14C, D, and E).

Figure 5.12A through C
Simulation of player hitting through shuttle

Figure 5.12A
Elbow is held at 9:00 position

Figure 5.12B
Contact with shuttle is made at 12:00

Figure 5.12C
Racket head follows through to 3:00

Figure 5.13A through E
Teaching of the forehand stroke

Figure 5.13A
Student is in basic stroke
position

Figure 5.13B
Instructor helps student begin
movement

Figure 5.13C
Instructor extends student's
racket-side arm

Figure 5.13D
Instructor points out position of racket
at contact

Figure 5.13E
Instructor makes sure that student's arm
follows through

**Figure 5.14A through E
Teaching of the backhand stroke**

**Figure 5.14A
Instructor has student assume
basic backhand stroke stance**

**Figure 5.14B
Instructor prepares to move
student's racket-side arm**

**Figure 5.14C
Instructor moves student's
arm through stroke**

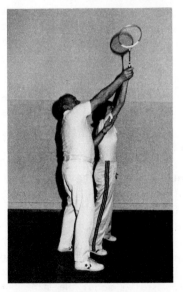

**Figure 5.14D
Instructor points out position
of racket at contact**

**Figure 5.14E
Instructor makes sure that student's
arm follows through**

LESSON 4: THE SINGLES SERVE—PUTTING SHUTTLE IN PLAY

I. **Preparation**

    A. Set up the courts.

    B. Have rackets and shuttles available for early arrivals.

II. **Content and Concepts**

    A. Physical Conditioning. Exercises can be led by the instructor or a student leader.

    B. Review and Warm-up. Following a brief review of the grip, ready position, and forehand and backhand strokes, students can practice while the instructor circulates and makes positive corrections as needed.

    C. The Singles Serve. Putting the shuttle in play involves an underhand stroke similar to the singles serve. Badminton rules require that a player's feet be in contact with the floor during a serve. This point should be emphasized during the explanation and practice session so that students can develop good habits. Table 5.4 outlines the procedures for assuming the stance and serving the shuttle.

    D. Teaching the Singles Serve. To teach the singles serve, as well as other skills, the instructor must develop a systematic approach.

        1. The procedures for teaching the singles serve are as follows:

            a. Arrange students at the side of the court so that each can easily see you.

            b. Explain and demonstrate serving the shuttle.

            c. Assign pairs of students to a court based on your evaluation of their skills.

            d. Give each pair six shuttles.

            e. Have each student stand about midcourt.

            f. Designate the student who will begin putting the shuttles into play.

            g. Have each student practice six serves.

            h. After practice, one student serves to a partner who, using the stroke just practiced, attempts to keep shuttle in play.

Table 5.4
Procedures for Assuming a Serving Stance and Stroking the Serve

The Stance	The Stroke
Stand erect	Drop shuttle from off-racket hand
Place off-racket foot forward, with toe pointed in direction the shuttle is to go	Shift weight from rear foot to front foot
Hold shuttle loosely between thumb and forefinger of off-racket hand	Swing racket downward and forward
Hold arm in front of and toward racket side of body	Turn thumb toward inside to bring racket face into proper hitting position
Hold racket arm back, with hand approximately at waist level and wrist cocked; now racket head is about the same height as shuttle	Uncock wrist so that at the point of contact arm is straight and racket head is perpendicular to the shuttle
Position racket-side arm so that racket can inscribe an arc downward and straight toward the partner	Contact shuttle approximately knee high and an arm's length in front of body; racket follows through, ending high over left shoulder

   i. When a shuttle goes out of play, the other player puts another into play.
   j. As students practice, circulate and make corrections as needed.

   2. Figure 5.15 shows an appropriate arrangement for practice involving 24 students. For 30 students, the perimeter of the court can be used. The usual arrangement for 16 students is four students to a court. The need for safety must be continually emphasized.

E. The analogy of the clock face applies. Properly executed, the singles serve stroke originates at 9:00, passes through 6:00, and ends as it passes through 3:00. Contact with the shuttle is made at approximately 3:30.

F. When shuttles are flying too high and short, the contact point is too high. When they fly too low and flat, the contact point is too far back toward the server.

LESSON 5: THE CLEAR

I. Preparation

A. Set up the courts.
B. Have rackets and shuttles available for early arrivals.

II. Content and Concepts

A. Physical Conditioning. Exercises can be led by the instructor or a student leader. Since a developmental approach is being used, the number and duration of exercises should be increased each week from this point on.

B. Review and Warm-up. Following a brief review of the singles serve, students can practice while the instructor circulates and makes positive corrections as needed.

C. The Clear. Using the chalkboard, the instructor defines and illustrates the clear.

   1. The clear can be a defensive or an offensive shot:

       a. Defensive. A defensive clear is sent high and deep into the opponent's court; the apex of flight is just short of the baseline and the shuttle falls straight down. It can be played from anywhere on the court, usually with an overhead stroke, and is used to regain a defensive position. The flight pattern is:

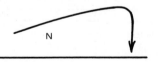

       b. Offensive. An offensive clear is used when the opponent is moving toward the net. It is an attacking stroke and should be hit with a flat trajectory that is just high enough so that the opponent can't reach it. The shuttle should land at the baseline. The flight pattern is:

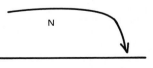

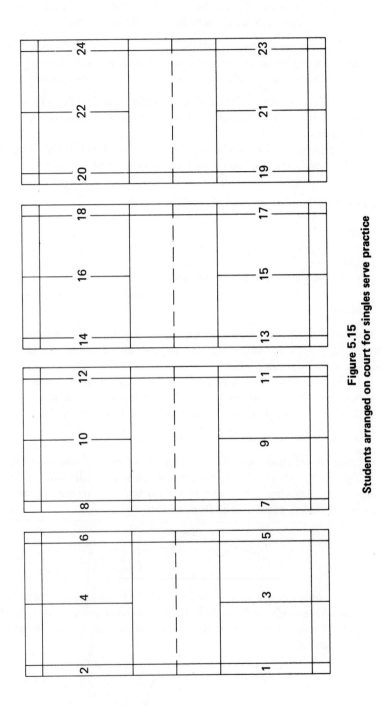

Figure 5.15
Students arranged on court for singles serve practice

2. The forehand clear is executed as follows:

   a. Take the same stance as that for the forehand stroke.
   b. Swing and attempt to contact the shuttle at a point above and about even with the racket-side shoulder. Contact with the shuttle should be at the highest point of the player's reach.
   c. Aim the shuttle high and deep so that it lands on or near the opponent's baseline. It is imperative in the beginning to strive for adequate length rather than height.

3. The backhand clear is executed as follows:

   a. Take the same stance as that for the backhand stroke.
   b. Bring the racket well back in preparation for stroke. Point the elbow upward.
   c. With a powerful upward and forward movement, meet the shuttle at the highest possible point.
   d. Keep the racket and racket-side arm in line with the shoulder.
   e. Strongly rotate the arm outward and extend the wrist to give speed to the racket head as well as to place the hitting surface of the racket in the proper position.

4. The procedures for practicing the clear are as follows:

   a. Students arrange themselves on the court as shown in Figure 5.16. Each should have three shuttles.
   b. Students 1 and 3 feed high shots to students 2 and 4 on the forehand and backhand. Students 2 and 4, utilizing correct stroke techniques, "clear" the shots high and deep so that they land on or near the X.

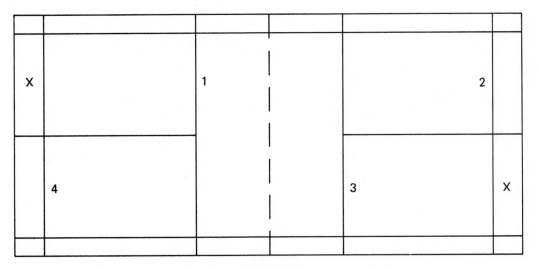

Figure 5.16
Students arranged on court for clear practice

    c. After six trials, students alternate positions.

    d. Once students show that they can stroke the shuttle reasonably well, they take positions in the middle of their end of the court. After putting the shuttle in play, students 1 and 2 and students 3 and 4 attempt to keep it in play by clearing to each other. As they gain control and can hit harder, they should keep moving back until they are able to clear from baseline to baseline.

III. Teaching Techniques and Aids

A. When students practice the clear off a serve, a partner should stand on the doubles long service line, with his or her racket outstretched. The player clearing the shuttle should hit it so that it drops straight down behind the partner. If three students are practicing, the rotation pattern shown in Figure 5.17 is used.

B. With the aid of additional standards, stretch a string across the floor (3 feet in from the baseline) at a height of 8 or 9 feet. This provides a target over which a defensive clear must go and shows the student whether the depth of the shot is adequate.

C. Certain procedures can help students having difficulty with the entire stroke. The teacher should instruct the student to:

    1. Assume the normal stroke position and extend the racket arm above the shoulder, with the wrist cocked.

    2. As shuttle approaches, use wrist action and arm rotation to strike the shuttle, with the racket following through.

    3. After practicing steps 1 and 2 assume normal hitting position, with the racket cocked behind the head. As shuttle approaches, extend arm, striking the shuttle.

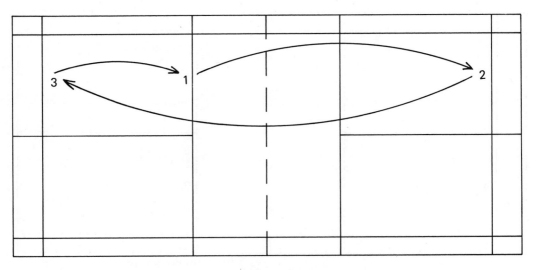

Figure 5.17
Rotation pattern when three students practice

4. Assume the next hitting position, placing weight on the rear foot and holding the racket back. Then transfer weight forward and strike the shuttle.
5. Begin at ready position and use the entire stroke.

D. The shuttle should be contacted at the highest possible point and as soon as possible. Therefore, students must go to the shuttle, which means controlling the play rather than letting the shuttle drop too low. To help students learn to reach, the instructor serves the shuttle to a player. As the shuttle reaches the apex of flight, the instructor says "swing." The player swings, hitting the shuttle at full extension. This technique calls for some judgment on the instructor's part and therefore must be practiced. Since most students still want to wait, they have to be instructed to swing when told, even though they believe the shuttle will be too high. This assumes that it is better to swing early, reach full extension, and miss the shot than to wait, bend the arm, and hit the shuttle. Timing comes with practice.

LESSON 6: THE DROP

I. Preparation

A. Set up the courts.
B. Have rackets and shuttles available for early arrivals.

II. Content and Concepts

A. Physical Conditioning. Exercises can be led by the instructor or a student leader.
B. Review and Warm-up. Following a brief review of the clear, students can practice while the instructor circulates and makes positive corrections as needed.
C. The Drop. Using the chalkboard, the instructor defines and illustrates the drop.

1. The drop shot causes the shuttle to drop steeply and close to the net in the opponent's forecourt. It is a finesse shot with the slowest flight of any basic shot. It is used to bring the opponent to the net and possibly force him or her to hit the shuttle *up* from below net level. It usually is hit with an overhead stroke to the corners of the opponent's court at the net. The flight pattern is:

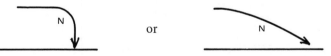

2. The procedures for executing the forehand overhead drop are as follows:

   a. Player uses same motion for the drop as for the clear, up to hitting range.
   b. The racket head passes through the hitting range at slow speed but with the arm at full extension in front of the body as contact is made with the shuttle at an angle approximately 45 degrees below the vertical.
   c. When contact is made, the racket must be over the shuttle and the stroke firmly made. Follow-through is the same as that for all overhead strokes.
   d. The shuttle must cross the net as close to the tape as possible.

3. For the drop to be effective, deceptive strategy must be employed. The strategy can take one of three forms:

  a. Overhead stroke, which makes the opponent think a clear or a smash is to be hit
  b. Horizontal stroke, which makes the opponent think a drive is to be hit
  c. Underhand stroke, which makes the opponent think a clear is to be hit

4. The procedures for practicing the overhead drop are as follows:

  a. Students 1 and 3 set up the shuttle for students 2 and 4 according to the procedures explained in step 3 of Lesson 5. Students 2 and 4 try to drop the shuttle just over the net and into the corners of the court indicated by X in Figure 5.18. After every six shots, students rotate positions.
  b. Students arrange themselves as shown in Figure 5.19. Student 2 sets up the shuttle for student 1, who alternately clears and drops it. Students 2 and 3 always clear to student 1. At rotation, student 1 takes the place of student 3, 2 replaces 1, and 3 replaces 2.

III. Teaching Techniques and Aids

  A. Outline various areas on the court so that students have a target at which to aim.
  B. Put standards together as shown in Figure 5.20. Strings outstretched across the court provide three zones through which the shuttle should pass. This gives students an accurate indication of how close the shuttle is to the net tape as it crosses the net.

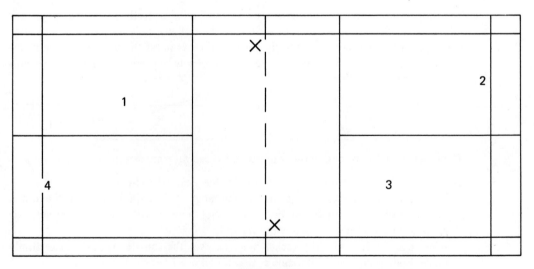

Figure 5.18
Arrangement of students on court for drop-shot practice

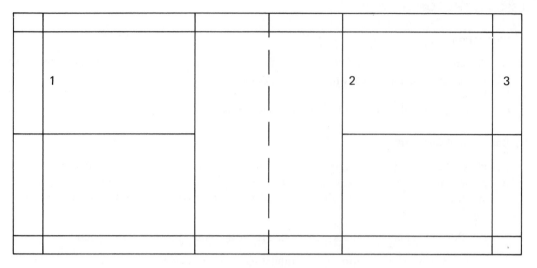

Figure 5.19
Students arranged on court for drop-clear practice

Figure 5.20
Court, net, and strings making targets for drop shot practice

LESSON 7: THE LOW SERVICE

I. Preparation

A. Prepare copies of Figure 5.21 showing the correct relationship of the racket to the hand during a serve.

B. Set up the courts.

C. Have rackets and shuttles available for early arrivals.

II. Content and Concepts

A. Physical Conditioning. Exercises can be led by the instructor or a student leader.

B. Review and Warm-up. Following a brief review of the drop, students can practice the clear and the drop while the instructor circulates, making positive corrections as needed.

C. The Low Service

1. Prior to explaining and demonstrating the low service, the instructor should:

    a. Stress the badminton rules stipulating that the racket must be pointed down discernibly and that the shuttle must be below the player's waist at point of contact. Also, the server and receiver must be within their proper courts and their feet must be in contact with the floor at time of service, i.e., when the racket contacts the shuttle (Figure 5.21).

    b. Point out that these rules make the service a defensive stroke. Proficiency is required to make the serve an offensive stroke.

2. The progression for teaching the low service is as follows:

    a. Assume a position approximately 2 feet behind the short service line.

    b. Place the off-racket foot slightly ahead of the racket-side foot.

    c. Point the toes of the off-racket foot at the opponent.

    d. Place the heel of the racket-side foot directly behind the off-racket heel, with the toes angled about 45 degrees toward the net.

    e. Rest weight slightly over the rear foot.

    f. Bring the racket arm back about waist high, with the elbow slightly bent and the arm relaxed. The racket head is up because of the cocked wrist. Use a modified forehand grip.

    g. Hold the shuttle between the thumb and forefinger of the off-racket hand, with the arm comfortably extended at shoulder height over a line that would extend from the racket-side foot.

    h. Prior to releasing the shuttle, sight the target area and net cords.

    i. Drop the shuttle merely by opening the finger and thumb. It should drop straight down.

    j. As the shuttle is dropped, simply let the racket arm swing the racket forward in a direct line to the shuttle. Watch the shuttle until it contacts the racket.

    k. The racket and shuttle should meet at a point approximately knee high and 2 feet in front of the racket-side foot. Keep the arm straight, with the wrist extended. The follow-through is relatively short.

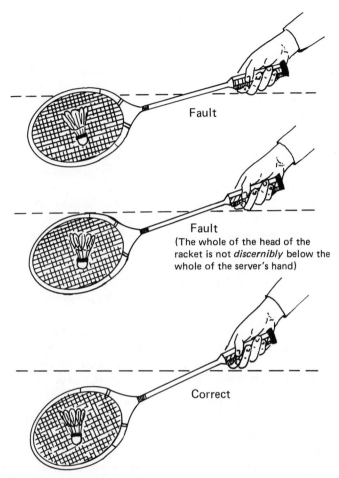

Positions of hand and racket at the instant of striking the shuttle

Figure 5.21
Delivery of service

Reproduced with permission of the United States Badminton Association from *Official Rules of Play*

l. Ease weight forward from the rear to the front foot as the service is executed.

m. Guide rather than hit the shuttle over the net.

n. The peak of the shuttle's flight is reached on the server's end of the court. Then the shuttle is descending as it crosses the net.

3. The procedures for practicing the low service are as follows:

a. Students arrange themselves as shown in Figure 4.2.

b. Each student serves six shuttles and then rotates positions.

c. The instructor circulates, making positive corrections as needed.

d. Since this is a static drill, additional markings can be put on the courts with tape (see Figure 4.2).

e. When a class is so large that there are extra people in spite of the procedure mentioned in step d, have students use the serving stations around the walls.*

III. Teaching Aids and Techniques

A. With the use of the standards described in Figure 3.2, target areas can be adjusted from 24 to 6 inches above the net. String can be stretched across all the courts at a given height. As the student's skill improves, the string can be lowered.

B. Some students step just before swinging (perhaps serving illegally). This can be corrected if they put their weight on the front foot prior to serving.

C. Have students mentally fix an *X* at the point where a simulated dropped shuttle will contact the racket. They should try to have the shuttle and racket meet at that point.

D. To demonstrate the flight of the shuttle, have each student hold the shuttle in the hand with the index finger inside the skirt (Figure 5.22). Beginning with the arm in the same position as it would be if the student were holding a racket, swing the arm forward and release the shuttle just beyond the vertical. If the shuttle flies too high, release is late; if it flies too low, release is early. When the racket is used, the contact point is approximately the same as the release point.

E. Teaching the low service may require the instructor to manually assist the student. It is important that the student realize that the arm action is similar to a pendulum. Also, the student must know that the arm should be held firm and straight and the wrist cocked back. Manual assistance consists of the following steps (Figure 5.23 A through D):

1. Student assumes the basic stance for low service.

2. Student holds the shuttle in the proper position with the racket held at shoulder height and the wrist cocked so that the racket is up.

*Data from unpublished research show that there is no significant difference in test results regardless of whether the student practices the low service with a net only, with a net and an overhead target area, or on the wall.

Figure 5.22
Preparing to toss shuttle across net

Figure 5.23A through D
Manual assistance

Figure 5.23A
Instructor prepares to manually assist
player through service

Figure 5.23B
Instructor assists player through service

Figure 5.23C
Instructor illustrates approximate point
of contact with shuttle

Figure 5.23D
Instructor makes sure that student's
arm follows through

3. Instructor stands alongside the student and grasps the back of the hand of his or her serving arm (Figure 5.23A).
4. Instructor manually moves the student's arm through the arc, emphasizing pendulum action and minimum wrist movement (Figure 5.23B and C).
5. Instructor attempts to have the student relax as the arm is moved back and forth to give the student the "feel" of the movement.
6. Instructor stops the racket at the point where contact with the shuttle should be made (Figure 5.23D).
7. Student drops the shuttle as the instructor manually moves the student's arm forward, attempting to contact the shuttle at the appropriate point.
8. Instructor emphasizes that the swing is from the 9:00 point through the downward arc to a point in front rather than from 6:00 upward.

LESSON 8: FOOTWORK

I. Preparation

A. Set up the courts.
B. Have rackets and shuttles ready for early arrivals.

II. Content and Concepts

A. Physical Conditioning. Exercises can be led by the instructor or a student leader.
B. Review and Warm-up. After a brief review of the low service, students can practice while the instructor circulates and makes corrections as needed.
C. Footwork. To cover the court well, the student must be able to move easily in all directions. This requires practice.

    1. Moving from home base toward sidelines. This movement is useful when replying to drives or to smashes hit down sidelines. Home base position is in the center of the court and is basic to singles play (Figure 5.24).

        a. The instructor should demonstrate movements in each direction from home base.
        b. Then students should practice. There can be three players on each end of the court. All should maintain a "bouncing" motion so that they can move quickly. This also helps keep their weight forward. The instructor then indicates in what direction students should move from home base and calls "Ready, move." The players stroke a simulated shuttle and return to home base to await the next call.

    2. Hitting forehand strokes while moving to sidelines

        a. Assume a ready position at home base.
        b. Take a short step with the racket-side foot toward the same sideline. Point this foot toward the sideline as it is put down.
        c. Take a crossover step with the off-racket foot, putting the body in the hitting position (Figure 5.25A and B).
        d. Cock the racket behind the head and make a simulated stroke.

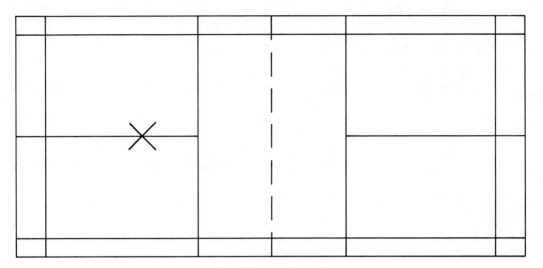

Figure 5.24
Location of home base

Figure 5.25A and B
Footwork when player moves to sidelines

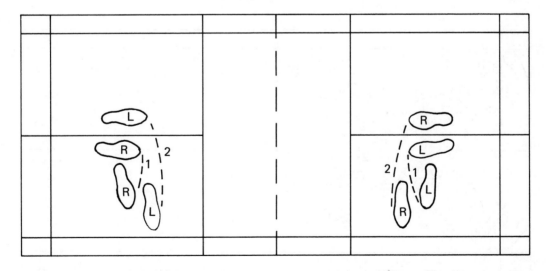

Figure 5.25A
Forehand for right-handed players

Figure 5.25B
Forehand for left-handed players

e. After stroking, push off with the off-racket foot and return it to its original position.

f. Shuffle or slide the racket-side foot to its original spot. Return to the ready position.

3. Hitting backhand strokes while moving to sidelines

   a. Assume a ready position at home base.

   b. Take a short step with the off-racket foot toward the same sideline, pointing the foot toward the sideline as it is put down.

   c. Take a crossover step with the racket-side foot, thus putting the body in the hitting position.

   d. Cock the racket at the off-racket shoulder and make a simulated stroke.

   e. After completing the stroke, push off with the racket-side foot and return it to its original position.

   f. Shuffle or slide the off-racket foot back to its original spot. Return to the ready position.

4. Moving from home base to corners. This movement is useful in replying to clears hit to the deep corners and drop shots hit to the corners of the forecourt. The star formation (Figure 5.26) is used because of points radiating from the center. Table 5.5 describes the procedures for executing the star drill.

   a. During practice, the player always begins at home base. In this drill, footwork is modified at the short forehand corner. It is important that the player be able to stop and stretch in order not to overrun the shot. Thus the lunge position (Figure 5.27) should be used. In this position, the racket-side foot bears the weight. The lower leg is perpendicular to the floor, and the thigh is at right angles to the lower left torso.

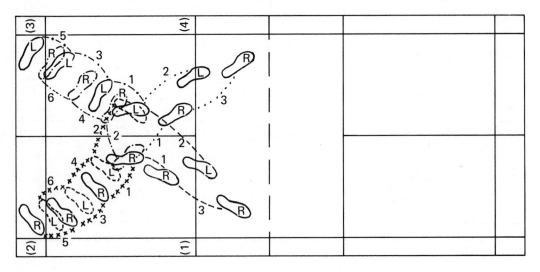

Figure 5.26
Footwork for star drill

Table 5.5
Procedures for Executing the Star Drill

1. Have player assume a ready position at home base
2. Instruct player to move as noted to each of the four corners:

Short Forehand Corner

a. Take short step forward with racket-side foot pointed in direction of the corner
b. Crossover with off-racket foot in the same direction, placing the foot on or about the short line
c. Bring racket-side foot forward, planting it in a position to support player's weight as racket is extended forward
d. Stroke simulated shuttle*
e. Push off with front foot and return to home base by placing front foot behind off-racket foot and taking sliding steps or short running steps

Deep Backhand Corner

a. Pivot on ball of racket-side foot and step toward the corner with off-racket foot
b. Continue to the back corner by bringing racket-side foot to off-racket foot; this procedure is repeated until off-racket foot is in back alley near baseline
c. Stroke simulated shuttle
d. Return to home base with short running steps beginning with off-racket foot

Deep Forehand Corner

a. Pivot on ball of off-racket foot and step in direction of the back corner with racket-side foot
b. Continue to the back corner by bringing off-racket foot to racket-side foot; this procedure is repeated until racket-side foot is in back alley close to baseline
c. Stroke simulated shuttle
d. Return to home base with short running steps beginning with racket-side foot

Short Backhand Corner

a. Crossover off-racket foot with racket-side foot in direction of the corner
b. Step in direction of the corner with off-racket foot
c. Step with racket-side foot toward corner, completing movement in the lunge position
d. Stroke simulated shuttle and push off with racket-side foot, returning to home base with short sliding steps or running steps

3. Demonstrate movements to each corner
4. Conduct practice session
   a. Have students walk through the drill first
   b. Have them run through the drill at slow speed
      (1) Concentrate on proper foot placement and technique
      (2) Gradually increase speed of the drill
   c. Each stroke must be made correctly; this helps player learn to assume proper position before stroking
   d. For drill purposes, player *must* pause at home base

*The same players may need to make another slight shuffle step if these moves do not place them in an appropriate stroking position. This is intended as a very basic approach. As students gain experience, it is possible to modify the techniques to fit individual characteristics.

Figure 5.27
The lunge position

The off-racket foot is in line with the racket-side foot; the inner side of the off-racket foot is against the floor.

  b. As practice, students should walk through the drill first. Then they should run through the drill at slow speed, concentrating on proper foot placement and technique and gradually increasing speed. Each stroke must be made correctly; this helps the player learn to assume the proper position before stroking. For drill purposes the player *must* pause at home base. Although these moves are learned in rotation, a player in an actual game may have to return to the spot from which he or she just came. Therefore, it is better not to allow a player to move directly from one corner to another. The instructor puts one student on each court and calls "Ready, move." Students should not complete more than three practice sets at full speed.

5. Moving from home base directly forward or backward. These movements are the same as those of the star drill except that the first steps are directly backward rather than to the corners.

  a. The instructor should demonstrate these movements.

  b. Then students should practice them. Since this is basically a straight-line drill, three students can work on each end of the court. The instructor arranges students on the court and calls "Ready, move."

LESSON 9: INTRODUCTION TO THE GAME

I. Preparation

    A. Draw a singles court on the chalkboard; the doubles court should be measured and ready to be drawn in.

    B. Have courts and shuttles ready for early arrivals.

II. Content and Concepts

    A. Physical Conditioning. Exercises can be led by the instructor or a student leader.

    B. Review and Warm-up. After a brief review of footwork procedures, students can practice while instructor circulates and makes corrections as needed.

    C. The Game. Students need a basic understanding of the rules and etiquette of badminton. Thus, the instructor must present the badminton rules summarized in Table 5.6 and explain them as necessary. Figure 5.28 is a diagram of a badminton court.

LESSON 10: THE DOUBLES GAME

I. Preparation

Arrange for a demonstration of a doubles game.

II. Content and Concepts

    A. Physical Conditioning. Exercises can be led by the instructor or a student leader.

    B. Review and Warm-up. After a brief review of the material presented to this point, students can practice while the instructor circulates and makes corrections as needed.

    C. The Doubles game. Before a demonstration game is played, the instructor can use the chalkboard to explain and demonstrate the concepts and the procedures involved in playing doubles.

        1. Doubles play involves these four basic concepts:

            a. Doubles is a team game in which each player must adjust to the strengths and weaknesses of a partner.

            b. Doubles is an attacking game in which one team attempts to put their opponents on the defensive.

            c. The system chosen (i.e., front-and-back, side-by-side, or a combination) depends on the strengths and weaknesses of each partner.

            d. A team should be in a front-and-back position when on the attack; in a side-by-side position when on the defensive.

        2. Serving is done in the following manner:

            a. The side having the first service in the game has only one opportunity to serve in its first inning; in subsequent innings each partner has a right to serve.

            b. When the serving side wins a point, the server then serves from the alternate court. This alternation continues until the side loses the right to serve.

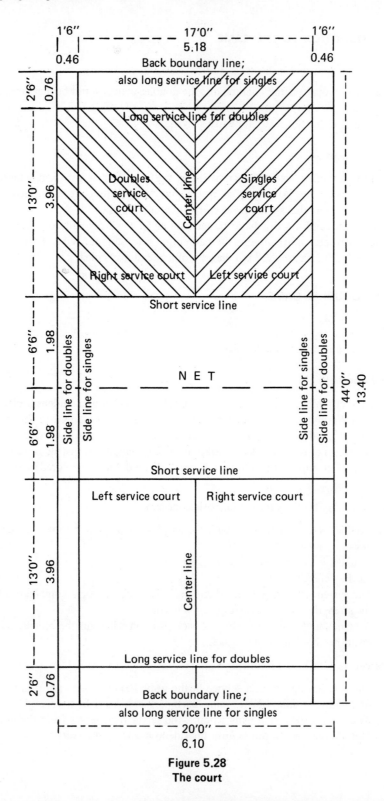

Figure 5.28
The court

Table 5.6
Summary of the Basic Rules of Badminton

The Court

Net—5 feet high at center; 5 feet 1 inch at posts
Singles court—17 feet by 44 feet
Doubles court—20 feet by 44 feet

The Players

Doubles—2 players per side
Singles—1 player per side

Starting the Game

Opposing sides toss; winner has option of

1. Serving first
2. Not serving first
3. Choosing ends

Side losing toss has choice of remaining options

Scoring

Doubles and men's singles—15 points
Women's singles—11 points
A game of 21 points may be arranged in doubles and men's singles

Changing Ends

Sides contest best 2 of 3 games usually
Sides change ends at beginning of game 2 and game 3 if necessary; also occurs in game 3 when leading score reaches:

8 in 15-point game
6 in 11-point game
11 in 21-point game

Setting

Setting is the process of extending score to win tied games; player or side reaching tied score first has option of setting

In 15-point game,13 all set to 5
14 all set to 3
In 11-point game, 9 all set to 3
10 all set to 2
In 21-point game,19 all set to 5
20 all set to 3

Decision to set must be made before the next service after the score has been tied
Side rejecting option may not be debarred from setting if a second opportunity arises

Faults

Fault by "in" side puts player out; by "out" side, yields a point.
Serving:

1. Striking shuttle higher than waist at point of contact
2. Head of racket above hand at point of contact
3. Shuttle falling in wrong service court, short, or out of bounds
4. Feet of server and receiver not in service court until service delivered
5. Player feints or balks opponent

Shuttle struck before crossing net
Player touches net when shuttle "in play"
Shuttle is thrown
Player hit by shuttle when standing out of bounds

Doubles Play

There are 2 sides: "in" side (serving side) and "out" side (receiving side)

One player of side beginning game entitled to serve in its first innings; in all subsequent innings each partner has right to serve; they serve consecutively

Player in right-hand service court of side winning toss begins game, serving to player diagonally opposite

If player served to puts shuttle in play, it will be hit alternately by each side until a fault is made or shuttle ceases to be in play

If point is won, server moves to left court and continues; as long as points are scored, process continues

If fault is made by "in" side, right to continue serving is lost; serve goes to partner or to other side

Player served to alone may return service

Table 5.6 *Continued*

Doubles Play

If receiver's partner plays or is hit by served shuttle, point for "in" side is made	If in the preceding cases side loses rally, mistake stands
If player serves out of turn or from wrong service court, side wins rally; call "Let," provided called before next service	Should player change sides inadvertently and mistake not be discovered until after next service, mistake stands and positions are not corrected
If player of receiving side is standing in wrong service court prepared to receive service, side wins rally, "Let"	

Singles Play

Player winning toss begins play in right service court	Players serve and receive in the right court only when score is 0 or even; in the left service court when score is odd
If opponent puts shuttle in play, hit alternately by each player until fault is made or shuttle ceases to be in play	Both players change service courts after each point has been scored

    c. The server's partner may stand anywhere as long as he or she does not obstruct or unsight an opponent.

    d. The server always serves into the court diagonally opposite.

    e. Players can determine if they are in the proper court for serving and receiving by remembering (1) that when the score is *even,* the person who began the game in the *right* court is always in the *right* court and (2) that when the score is *odd,* the person who began the game in the *right* court is in the *left* court.

III. Teaching Techniques and Aids

    A. As the demonstration game progresses, the instructor points out all items of importance covered during the explanation.

    B. Following the demonstration, students should return to their courts and play as long as time permits. The instructor circulates, answers questions, and corrects errors as needed.

    C. When a class is large, students can be arranged on the court as shown in Figure 5.29. They should note exactly where they are standing. The instructor should time the game so that no player plays longer than another. At the end of each time period, the instructor directs players to rotate one position counterclockwise and begin another game.

LESSON 11: DOUBLES SYSTEM

I. Preparation

Draw three diagrams of courts on the chalkboard.

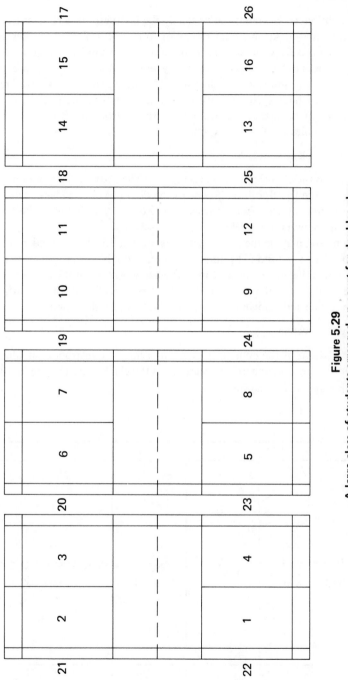

Figure 5.29
A large class of students arranged on court for doubles play

II. Content and Concepts

A. Physical Conditioning. Exercises can be led by the instructor or a student leader.

B. Review and Warm-up. After a brief review of footwork drills and the low service, students can practice these skills while the instructor circulates and makes corrections as needed.

C. Doubles Systems. For beginning classes two systems of doubles play are presented: the front-and-back system and the side-by-side system (Figure 5.30). Since areas of responsibility are clearly defined in both systems, both can be used by beginners. Since winning is not the goal, it is recommended that mixed doubles use the front-and-back system and that men's and women's doubles use the side-by-side system.

   1. Front-and-back system

      a. The division of the court is the short line. The instructor should shade in the division line and the front position on one of the diagrams on the chalkboard (Figure 5.30).
      b. The person playing front is responsible for the area between the short line and the net and between the sidelines.
      c. The person playing the backcourt is responsible for the remainder of the court.
      d. This system is used (1) primarily in mixed doubles, (2) when one partner is strong but not very good at the net, and (3) when a team is on the attack.
      e. The weakness of the system is that the person playing the backcourt can be run from side to side and a down-the-line smash is not easily defended.

   2. Side-by-side system

      a. The division of the court is at the centerline. The instructor should shade in the appropriate area on one of the diagrams on the chalkboard (Figure 5.30).
      b. Each player plays one side only.

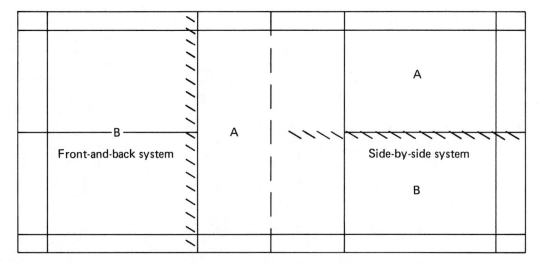

Figure 5.30
Divisions of badminton court for both systems of doubles play

c. The forehand plays shots down the middle.

d. If the team has a left-handed and a right-handed player, the better backhand plays shots down the middle. This decision is made at the beginning of the game.

e. This system is used when the team is on the defensive.

f. The weakness of the system is that the weak player can be played all the time.

III. Teaching Techniques and Aids

A. When playing mixed doubles, the woman should play the forecourt and the man the backcourt.

B. When the man is serving, the woman stands on the short line 2 to 3 feet from the centerline, depending on the service court.

C. The instructor announces pairings for the day, circulates and helps students understand the system being played, and begins evaluation of each student at play.

LESSON 12: THE SMASH

I. Preparation

Prepare the day's pairings for doubles play.

II. Content and Concepts

A. Physical Conditioning. Exercises can be led by the instructor or a student leader.

B. Review and Warm-up. After a brief review of doubles play, students can practice while the instructor circulates and makes corrections as needed.

C. The Smash. Using the chalkboard, the instructor defines and illustrates the smash.

1. The smash is a powerful overhead stroke that directs the shuttle sharply downward; it is the point-winning shot in the game. The flight pattern is:

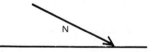

The smash is used whenever possible in doubles and whenever there is a chance of winning a point in singles. Its success depends on racket head speed and angle of the shot. Angle depends on the player's position on the court. The racket must be over the shuttle when contact is made. The shuttle should be hit at the sharpest possible angle and aimed directly at the opponent, aimed away from the opponent, or hit so hard that the opponent can't handle it.

2. The procedures for executing the forehand smash are as follows:

a. Preliminary movements are the same as those for all other shots.

b. Weight is transferred from the rear foot to the front foot as the stroke is made.

c. The shuttle is contacted in front of and to the racket side of the player's head; the exact point of contact depends on the player's position on the court.

d. Inward rotation of the arm and snapping of the wrist through the hitting range brings the racket over the top of the shuttle, thus ensuring that it is hit down.

e. Pace is the most important element at this level; as defense improves, placement acquires greater importance.

f. Proper execution depends on proper footwork, proper balance, and proper timing.

g. Follow-through is the same as that for all overhead strokes.

3. The procedures for practicing the smash are as follows:

a. The staggered formation shown in Figure 5.31 is used.

b. Players 1 and 3 stand on or just behind the short service line, while players 2 and 4 take a position at midcourt.

c. Players 1 and 3 serve six shuttles high and to the racket side of players 2 and 4.

d. Players 2 and 4 practice hitting on top of the shuttle to direct it downward.

e. After every six shots, players rotate positions.

III. Teaching Techniques and Aids

A. When teaching the smash, the instructor should present it in the order given below to those who have difficulty.

1. Have the student assume basic stroke position with the racket-side arm held up, wrist cocked.

2. The shuttle is hit up to the player, who then moves the arm forward, rotates it inward, and snaps the wrist so that the racket hits the shuttle on top and directs it downward.

3. After the student achieves a degree of proficiency with this process, have him or her start with the racket cocked behind his or her head.

4. Have the shuttle set up and have the student, moving the arm only, meet the shuttle in front of his or her body, with the racket on top directing the shuttle downward.

5. Since the swing takes more time, it must begin earlier to contact the shuttle at the same point.

6. After the student gains proficiency, have him or her begin at the ready position and use the complete stroke.

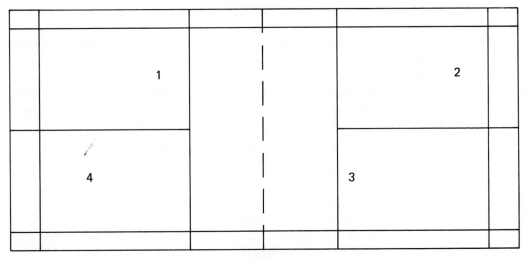

Figure 5.31
Staggered formation for smash practice

B. Manual assistance, discussed in Lesson 3, can also be used here. Only the contact point differs.

LESSON 13: THE DRIVE

I. Preparation

A. Set up the courts.
B. Have rackets and shuttles ready for early arrivals.

II. Content and Concepts

A. Physical Conditioning. Exercises can be led by the instructor or a student leader.
B. Review and Warm-up. After a brief review of the smash, students can practice while the instructor circulates and makes corrections as needed.
C. The Drive. Using the chalkboard, the instructor defines and illustrates the drive.

    1. The drive shot travels parallel to the floor and crosses the net very close to the tape. The flight pattern is:

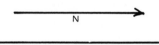

    The drive is useful in doubles against a front-and-back system. It usually is hit down the line and lands at midcourt or beyond. The drive should be hit crosscourt only when it might go between partners standing diagonally on the court—it is seldom used this way. When hit, the drive should be aimed directly at an opponent, toward an unguarded spot, or between the players in doubles. Table 5.7 provides a comparison of the clear, drop, smash, and drive.

    2. The procedures for executing the forehand drive are as follows:

      a. Assume a ready position.
      b. Pivot on the racket-side foot and bring the racket back behind the head.
      c. Transfer weight from the rear foot to the front foot as stroke is begun.
      d. Contact shuttle well in front of the body, in front of the shoulder, with the arm extended, and the racket head perpendicular to the flight path of the shuttle.
      e. Determine the amount of power needed by position on the court.
      f. To get more power, turn back more toward the net, pointing the off-racket foot more toward the sidelines.
      g. Prolong follow-through when more power is needed.

    3. The procedures for executing the backhand drive are as follows:

      a. Assume a ready position.
      b. Pivot on the off-racket foot and bring the racket back in preparation.
      c. Transfer weight from the rear foot to the front foot as stroke is begun.
      d. Contact shuttle well in front of the body opposite the racket-side shoulder, with the arm extended and the racket head perpendicular to the shuttle.
      e. Determine the amount of power needed by position on the court.
      f. To get more power, position the back more toward the net, with the racket-side foot pointing toward the sidelines.

Table 5.7
Comparison of the Clear, Drop, Smash, and Drive

	Clear	Drop	Smash	Drive
Definition				
Defensive	Shot sent high and deep into opponent's court; apex of flight just short of baseline; shuttle falls straight down	Shot causes shuttle to drop steeply and close to net in opponent's forecourt; finesse shot; has slowest flight of any basic shot	Powerful overhead stroke that directs shuttle sharply downward; it is the main point-winning shot in game	Shot that travels parallel to floor and crosses net very close to tape
Offensive	Used when opponent moving toward net; shuttle's flight pattern flat and just high enough so that opponent can't reach it; shuttle should land at baseline			
Use	On defensive, enables player to gain time to reestablish a defensive position On offensive, serves as an attacking stroke if opponent can be caught off guard (i.e., moving toward net)	On defensive, brings opponent to net On offensive, possibly forces opponent to hit shuttle up from below net level	Whenever possible in doubles; primarily when there is a good chance of winning a point in singles	Most useful in doubles against a front-and-back system; usually lands at midcourt or beyond; should be hit crosscourt only when it might go between partners standing diagonally on court—seldom used this way
Stroke	Can be played from anywhere on court with either stroke; most commonly hit overhead	Can be played from any position on court; can cross net at any point, but preferably at corners	Must be hit at sharpest possible angle; should be aimed directly at opponent, aimed away from opponent, or hit so hard that opponent can't handle it	Should be aimed directly at opponent, toward an unguarded spot past opponent, or between players in doubles
Flight pattern				
Defensive				
Offensive				

4. After the instructor demonstrates the drive, students can go to their courts to practice.

III. Teaching Techniques and Aids

A. To practice, students are arranged in the following way:

1. Players 1 and 2 and players 3 and 4 stand in the center of their respective courts (Figure 5.32).
2. The four players practice driving the shuttle back and forth, always down the line, emphasizing improving technique before increasing power.

B. The same standards and string used for the low service can provide targets or zones through which students can attempt to hit the shuttle.

LESSON 14: NET PLAY

I. Preparation

A. Set up the courts.
B. Have rackets and shuttles ready for early arrivals.

II. Content and Concepts

A. Physical Conditioning. Exercises can be led by the instructor or a student leader.
B. Review and Warm-up. After a brief review of the drive, students can practice while the instructor circulates and makes corrections as needed.

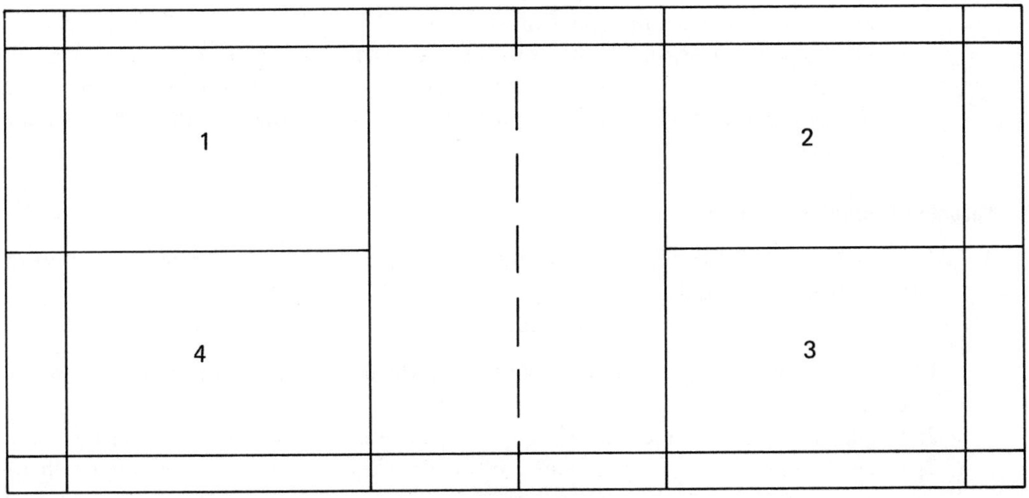

Figure 5.32
Students arranged on court for drive practice

C. Net Play

1. This type of play takes place between the short service line and the net. Also defined as hairpins or crosscuts, these delicate shots cross the net very close to the tape.
2. The procedures for executing net shots are as follows:

   a. Use a forehand grip.
   b. Hold the racket lightly but in a controlled way in the fingers; touch should be delicate but firm.
   c. Use open or backhand stance with the off-racket foot placed close to short service line. This enables the off-racket foot to be the pivot foot, which allows good coverage from a single position.
   d. Meet the shuttle as close to the top of the net cord as possible.
   e. Angle the face of the racket toward the area of the court at which the shuttle is directed.
   f. Be sure that wrist movement is limited but firm.
   g. If the racket can or will contact the shuttle at the *top of the cord,* place the racket head parallel to the net cord and let the shuttle drop onto the racket and rebound just over the net. This is particularly useful if the shuttle is dropping vertically close to the net and the player is in doubt as to whether the shuttle will drop on his or her side of the net.
   h. When the shuttle hits the net cord and is tumbling, wait until its flight path straightens out before attempting to play the shot.

3. Net shots are used when the opponent is out of position and the shuttle is dropping too close to the net for a flick clear. The instructor can explain strategy using Figures 5.33 and 5.34:

   a. Play to point A when the opponent is at point C.
   b. Play to point B when the opponent is at point D.
   c. Play to points A, B, and C when the opponent is in shaded area.
   d. A player with good technique and confidence can engage an opponent in a game at the net. It is possible to play to point A when the opponent is there, but the shot must be precise.

III. Teaching Techniques and Aids

A. After the instructor's demonstration of net shots, students can take their positions on the short service line for practice.
B. As students practice, the instructor should:

1. Emphasize that students should keep the racket up and meet the shuttle at the net cord.
2. Emphasize that they should try to keep the shuttle as close to the net cord as possible.
3. Circulate and correct errors, the most obvious problem at this time being too much arm or wrist action.

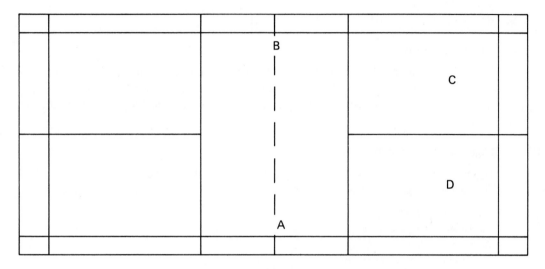

Figure 5.33
Targets for net shots when opponent is in or toward backcourt

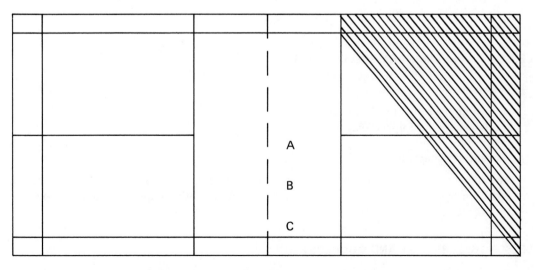

Figure 5.34
Targets for net shots when opponent is in shaded area

LESSONS 15 AND 16: REVIEW

I. Preparation

A. Set up the courts.
B. Have rackets and shuttles ready for early arrivals.

II. Content and Concepts

A. Physical Conditioning. Exercises can be led by the instructor or a student leader.
B. Review and Warm-up. Since students have had to assimilate quite a lot of new material, a comprehensive review is beneficial at this time. Refer to individual lessons for specific procedures.

III. Teaching Techniques and Aids

A. To make appropriate corrections, an instructor must be able to spot errors being committed. The following are common faults:

  1. Hurried stroking
  2. Crowding the shuttle
  3. Overreaching
  4. Taking the shuttle too low
  5. Checking the follow-through
  6. Allowing grip to slip
  7. Taking eyes off the shuttle
  8. Holding the racket face at wrong angle
  9. Using incorrect footwork
  10. Locking the wrist

B. Instructor should make corrections in a positive manner.

LESSON 17: PRELIMINARY SKILLS TESTS

I. Preparation

A. Set up the courts for the low service and clear tests.
B. Prepare forms for recording test scores.

II. Content and Concepts

To administer the low service and clear tests, the instructor divides the class in half. Group 1 is tested on the low service and group 2 on the clear. When both groups have finished, they take the other test.

LESSON 18: STRATEGY AND DOUBLES PLAY

I. Preparation

Prepare a series of badminton court diagrams on the chalkboard for use in discussing strategy.

II. Content and Concepts

A. Physical Conditioning. Exercises can be led by the instructor or a student leader.

B. Understanding the Game. Once students can perform the basic shots of badminton, they must learn the game of badminton. This involves overall strategy and knowing how to benefit from an opponent's weakness.

1. Strategy is the process of using shots in a deliberate way either to win a point or to take the service from the opponent. It begins with the game's first serve—or even earlier. With each stroke, the player wants to play the shuttle into the opponent's court in a way that (1) prevents the opponent from making a dangerous return or (2) forces the opponent to miss a return or make a weak return that gives the player a chance to make a decisive stroke.

2. Weaknesses in badminton are of two kinds: those common to all players (such as shots hit to the deep backhand) and those peculiar to the individual. Table 5.8 lists common weaknesses and the best option for handling them. However, the instructor should stress that for any strategy to be effective, a player must *always* know (a) the position of the opponent and (b) the position of the lines.

3. Players should consider the following maxims when hitting:

    a. Hit to the part of the court where the opponent can do the least.
    b. Hit to weak points.
    c. Hit away from the opponent.
    d. Hit to an area where the opponent does not expect it.
    e. Hit so hard that the opponent cannot see the shuttle clearly.
    f. Attempt to break up the opposing combination or play to the weakest opposing partner.
    g. Maintain own combination.

4. The choice of returns to an opponent's shot depends on the degree of perfection of the shot. For example, in Table 5.9, the first choice of a return to a low service is a smash. The assumption is that the service is poorly done and can be smashed. When the service is well done, a clear or a net shot is an alternative. Table 5.9 shows various shots and their possible replies.

Table 5.8
Player Weaknesses and Shot Options

Weakness	Option
A weak backhand	Keep hitting to that side
A weak clear	Keep hitting deep
A weakness in handling drop shots	Keep dropping
Slowness	Keep player moving
Deep receiving service	Keep serving short
Serving from up close	Return deep

Table 5.9
Possible Returns to Various Shots by Opponent

Opponent's Shot	Choice of Returns			
	First	Second	Third	Fourth
Low service	Smash	Clear	Net	
Long service	Smash	Clear	Drop	Drive
Drive	Drop	Clear	Drive	
Clear	Smash	Clear	Drive	
Clear	Smash	Clear	Drop	Drive
Net shot	Smash	Clear	Cross-court	Hairpin
Drop	Smash	Net shot	Clear	
Smash	Drop	Clear		

III. Teaching Techniques and Aids

A. Play that begins at this point is designed to help the instructor in the final evaluation of each student.

B. A competitive schedule based on random numbers (Appendix B) permits the instructor to pair students in a random fashion, thus removing any possible bias.

C. In doubles play, the instructor reassigns partners at a regular interval so that students have the opportunity to play with and adjust to different partners.

D. Play is designed to give students competitive practice without having to win.

LESSON 19: THE SINGLES SERVE—STRATEGY

I. Preparation

A. Set up the courts.

B. Have rackets and shuttles ready for early arrivals.

II. Content and Concepts

A. Physical Conditioning. Exercises can be led by the instructor or a student leader.

B. Review and Warm-up. Students can continue doubles play while the instructor circulates and makes corrections as needed.

C. The Singles Serve

1. The procedures for executing the singles serve listed in Lesson 4 should be reviewed. The instructor should emphasize and demonstrate that a singles serve must be high and deep. Flight characteristics are the same as those for the clear.

2. The procedures for practicing the singles serve are as follows:

a. Students arrange themselves on the court as shown in Figure 5.35.

b. Students 2 and 4 stand on the doubles long service line, with the racket raised over the head.

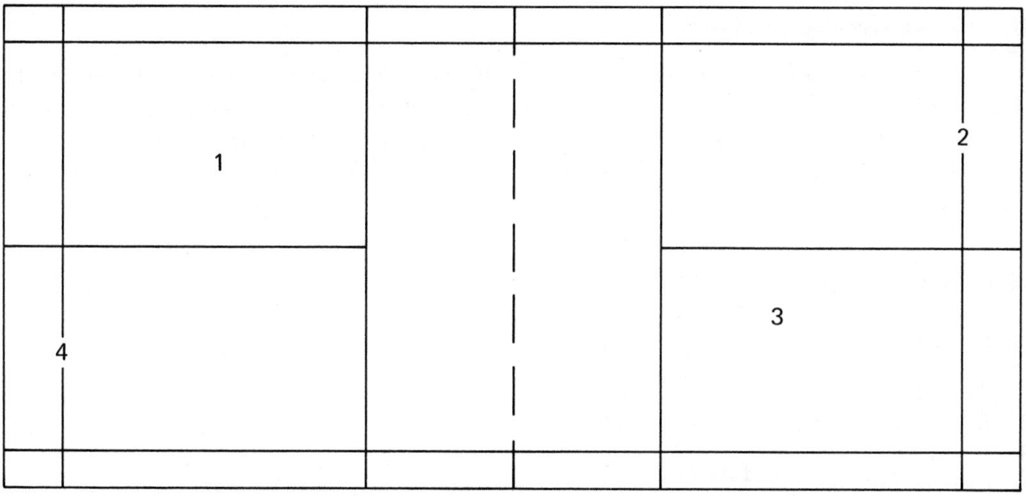

Figure 5.35
Students arranged on court for singles serve practice

   c. Students 1 and 3 attempt to serve the shuttle high and deep so that it lands behind the partner.

   d. At the end of six serves, partners change positions.

III. Teaching Techniques and Aids

Tape or string can be stretched across the courts so that the zone becomes a target.

LESSON 20: THE SINGLES GAME

I. Preparation

Arrange for a demonstration game of singles.

II. Content and Concepts

  A. Physical Conditioning. Exercises can be led by the instructor or a student leader.

  B. The Singles Game

    1. The following concepts pertain in singles play:

      a. A singles player depends on quickness, agility, deception, and physical condition.

      b. The singles game calls for accurate clears, good drop shots, good net play, and good movement.

    2. As a demonstration game of singles is played, the instructor should point out the:

      a. Depth of the service

      b. Placement of the service

      c. Choice of shots for moving the opponent around the court

      d. Infrequent use of the smash

III. Teaching Techniques and Aids

A. After the demonstration game, a group of students plays a singles game and the rest practice the low service against the wall. After a predetermined time limit, students reverse positions. This process is continued until all students have played a singles game.

B. Doubles play also is continued as scheduled. The instructor circulates, corrects errors, and evaluates students.

LESSONS 21 through 25: PLAY

I. Preparation

A. Set up the courts.

B. Have rackets and shuttles available for early arrivals.

II. Content and Concepts

A. Physical Conditioning. Exercises can be led by the instructor or a student leader.

B. Review and Warm-up

1. Doubles play is continued as scheduled.
2. Singles play continues.
3. Students not scheduled to play should practice the low service on the wall.

LESSON 26: LOW SERVICE TEST

I. Preparation

A. Prepare the courts and record sheets for the low service test (see Chapter 8).

B. Obtain 12 new shuttles and one good racket.

C. Prepare a double elimination tournament for singles and doubles.

II. Content and Concepts

While one group is being tested, the other students begin the tournament. Tournament games should be 21 points each.

III. Teaching Techniques and Aids

Test the top half of the doubles bracket first; then test the bottom half.

LESSON 27: CLEAR TEST

I. Preparation

A. Prepare the courts for the clear test.

B. Make available the same shuttles and racket used for the low service test.

II. Content and Concepts

A. Administer the clear test (Chapter 8).
B. Continue the tournament.

III. Teaching Techniques and Aids

Administer the clear test. The procedures are the same as those used for the low service test.

LESSON 28: PHYSICAL FITNESS TESTS

I. Preparation

A. Prepare the courts and record sheets for whatever tests are to be given.
B. Secure the proper equipment.

II. Content and Concepts

A. Administer the physical fitness tests.
B. Continue the tournament.

III. Teaching Techniques and Aids

Administer the physical fitness tests. Use the same procedures discussed in Lesson 26.

LESSON 29: MAKEUP TESTS

I. Preparation

Prepare the courts for the administration of tests.

II. Content and Concepts

A. Provide makeup test opportunities.
B. Continue the tournament.

III. Teaching Techniques and Aids

A. Administer makeup tests as needed.
B. Complete the tournament.

LESSON 30: WRITTEN EXAMINATION

I. Preparation

Prepare the examinations.

II. Content and Concepts

    A. Administer written examination to obtain a final evaluation of each student's knowledge of badminton.

    B. At the conclusion of classes, inventory the equipment, destroying all broken shuttles and repairing broken strings in rackets, and store equipment in its proper place.

STUDENT PROJECT

Based on the information presented in Chapters 2 and 5, prepare a class handout sheet on course requirements, operating procedures for the course, or course objectives.

6

Teaching
Intermediate Badminton

Beginning classes in badminton are designed to give students a sound stroke base, the ability to demonstrate basic shots, and a basic knowledge of the strategy and rules of badminton. Intermediate classes are designed to reinforce the fundamentals, to teach new skills, and to increase knowledge of the strategy and rules of badminton. In intermediate badminton, greater emphasis is placed on winning competitive games; however, the ability of a player to adjust to a partner is still paramount.

The results of the low service and clear tests plus a subjective evaluation of ability are used by the instructor to assign partners of approximately equal ability. These results also serve to measure degree of improvement. The organization of lessons is essentially the same as that for beginning badminton (see Chapter 5); modifications are noted as necessary.

LESSON 1: ORIENTATION

I. Preparation

    A. Have handouts ready.
    B. Bring samples of rackets and shuttles and a list of prices.

II. Content and Concepts

    A. Orientation

        1. Ascertain students' playing experience and any possible medical restrictions.
        2. Show samples of rackets and shuttles to students, pointing out characteristics and advantages of each as well as the comparative price. Some students may want to buy their own racket.

    B. Evaluation. After completing orientation, the instructor should:

        1. Assign students temporarily to courts and have them hit together.
        2. Carry out a subjective evaluation to be used together with skills test scores to assign students permanent partners.

III. Teaching Techniques and Aids

The instructor may find a local sports equipment dealer who would be willing to visit the class and exhibit badminton equipment.

LESSON 2: PRELIMINARY LOW SERVICE TEST

I. Preparation

A. Bring handouts.
B. Check any medical restrictions of new students.
C. Set up the courts for the low service test.
D. Prepare the forms for recording test scores.

II. Content and Concepts

A. Physical Conditioning. Exercises can be led by the instructor or a student leader.
B. Administration of Low Service Test.

   1. When giving the low service test, the instructor can refer to Chapter 5, Lesson 26, and to Chapter 8, page 126.
   2. Students not directly involved in testing during the class period should practice with each other.

LESSON 3: PRELIMINARY CLEAR TEST

I. Preparation

A. Bring handouts.
B. Check any medical restrictions of new students.
C. Set up the courts for the clear test.
D. Prepare the forms for recording test scores.

II. Content and Concepts

A. Physical Conditioning. Exercises can be led by the instructor or a student leader.
B. Administration of Clear Test.

   1. When administering the clear test, the instructor can refer to Chapter 5, Lesson 27, and to Chapter 8, page 130.
   2. Students not directly involved in testing during the class period can practice with each other.

LESSON 4: REVIEW—THE GRIP AND STROKING

I. Preparation

A. Have the grip templates ready for class (refer to Chapter 5, Lesson 2).

B. Set up the courts.

C. Have rackets and shuttles available for early arrivals.

II. Content and Concepts

A. Physical Conditioning. Exercises can be led by the instructor or a student leader.

B. Reviews. A review of previously learned skills is a routine part of any physical education progression and makes those skills a permanent part of the movement pattern. Reviews always make a positive presentation possible.

1. Review the forehand grip (Chapter 5, Lesson 2). Then students practice assuming the grip while the instructor circulates and makes corrections as needed.

2. Review the backhand grip (Chapter 5, Lesson 2). After a brief review of the procedure for changing from the forehand to a backhand grip, students practice while instructor circulates and makes corrections as needed.

3. Review the ready position (Chapter 5, Lesson 3). Then students practice the stance as the instructor circulates and makes corrections as needed.

4. Review the basic forehand stroke position (Chapter 5, Lesson 3). Then students practice stroking a simulated shuttle at all levels.

5. Review the basic backhand stroke position (Chapter 5, Lesson 3). Then students practice stroking a simulated shuttle at all levels.

C. Overhead Strokes Against the Wall

1. With students sitting in a line perpendicular to the wall and facing the racket side of the instructor, the instructor explains and demonstrates, using the wall, the overhead stroke on the forehand. For the demonstration on the backhand, students should face the off-racket side of the instructor.

2. The speed with which the shuttle rebounds and the distance it flies depend on the force with which it is hit. When the shuttle is hit hard, the rebound is fast. Because of the speed of the rebound, the student must be able to prepare for the next stroke quickly. Thus, the student cannot afford a long, slow follow-through.

3. The procedures for executing a forehand overhead stroke against the wall are as follows:

   a. Stand approximately 6 feet from the wall in a serving stance.

   b. Serve the shuttle high (approximately 10 feet, and as it rebounds, assume the basic stroke position, quickly readying the racket.

   c. As the shuttle descends, hit an overhead stroke and keep the shuttle in play.

   d. Emphasize quick wrist action, inward rotation of the arm, full extension, short follow-through, and immediate preparation for the next stroke.

   e. Whether the shuttle and racket are perpendicular at contact can be determined as the player strokes. When the racket strikes the shuttle squarely, the rebound is straight because the shuttle came off the racket straight. If the shuttle travels to the off-racket side, the racket head was open, i.e.:

If the shuttle travels to the racket side, the racket head was closed, i.e.:

4. The procedures for executing a backhand overhead stroke against the wall are as follows:

   a. Stand approximately 6 feet from the wall in a serving stance.
   b. Serve the shuttle high (approximately 10 feet), directing it toward the off-racket side. As the shuttle rebounds, take a backhand stroke position, quickly readying the racket.
   c. As the shuttle descends, hit an overhead stroke, keeping the shuttle in play.
   d. Emphasize good preparation, speed of the outward rotation of the arm and wrist snap, short follow-through, and return to a preparatory stance.
   e. Again, the player knows that the racket is square to the shuttle if the shuttle comes off the racket straight. If the shuttle goes toward the racket side, the racket face was open, i.e.:

If the shuttle goes toward the off-racket side, the racket face was closed, i.e.:

D. Practice. Students take a shuttle, spread out, and practice stroking against the wall while the instructor circulates and corrects errors as needed.

III. Teaching Aids and Techniques

A. When students are learning the grip, the conformation of the handle is strange to them. Therefore, they have to look at it to take the grip. To help students develop the appropriate "feel," the instructor should:

   1. Point out that the handle is eight-sided (see Figure 3.5), with the sides parallel to the hitting surface being wider than the others. The two sides in line with the frame are slightly smaller. Beveled edges connect these four surfaces.
   2. Remind students that the "V" of the thumb and forefinger is over the side in line with the head.
   3. To determine if the students really know the grip, have them grip the racket, close their eyes, twist the racket in their hands, and assume the correct grip without looking at the racket.
   4. Have them attempt this several times.

B. Stimuli are either internal or external. One of the steps in developing skill is improving the capacity for self-analysis. Internalizing stimuli helps in this process.

   1. One approach to internalization is to have the student close his or her eyes and project upon that dark area the image of the instructor demonstrating a movement such as an overhead stroke. Then have the student project upon that image the form as the student

perceives it. Where these images coincide, the movement is considered correct; where they do not, corrections must be made.

2. This is a difficult but often worthwhile procedure.

LESSON 5: REVIEW—THE CLEAR AND DROP

I. Preparation

A. Assign students to partners and courts on the basis of test scores and informal evaluation.
B. Set up the courts.
C. Have rackets and shuttles available for early arrivals.

II. Content and Concepts

A. Physical Conditioning. Exercises can be led by the instructor or a student leader.
B. Review

    1. Review the clear (Chapter 5, Lesson 5). Then students practice while the instructor circulates and makes corrections as needed.
    2. Review the drop (Chapter 5, Lesson 6). Then students practice while the instructor circulates and makes positive corrections as needed.

C. Practice

    1. Using the staggered formation shown in Figure 6.1 on each court have student 2 serve the shuttle to student 1, who alternately drops and clears to students 2 and 3. After 10

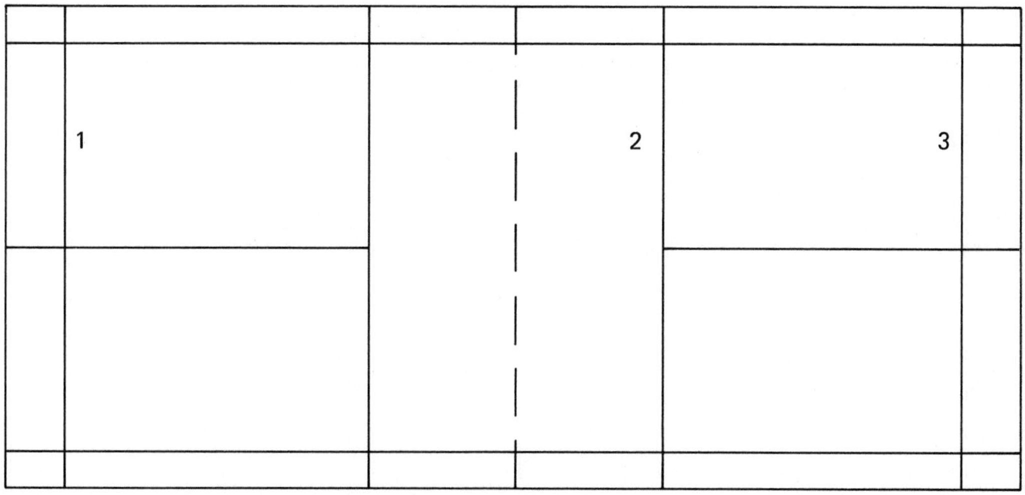

Figure 6.1
Students arranged on court for clear-drop practice

strokes, students rotate positions, i.e., student 2 takes the place of student 1, 3 replaces 2, and 1 replaces 3.

2. Using the staggered formation with three players on each side of the court shown in Figure 6.2, have student 2 serve to student 1, who clears to student 3; 3 drops to 5, who clears to 4; 4 clears to 6, who drops to 2, who begins the entire process again. After 10 strokes, each player rotates one position in a clockwise direction.

D. Underhand Strokes Against the Wall

1. The same arrangement as that described in Lesson 4 is used. The instructor explains that practicing underhand strokes against the wall develops quick reflexes, reactions, and wrist action and then demonstrates these strokes.

2. The procedures for executing underhand strokes against the wall are as follows:

  a. Assume a forehand stroke position about 5 feet from the wall.
  b. Place the shuttle in play by serving the shuttle against the wall.
  c. Keep the shuttle in play by maintaining a bouncing motion on the balls of the feet, by using a short backswing, always with the wrist cocked, and by quickly snapping the racket through the shot.
  d. This fast action requires the player to adjust to a backhand stance as the situation demands and then quickly return to a forehand stance.

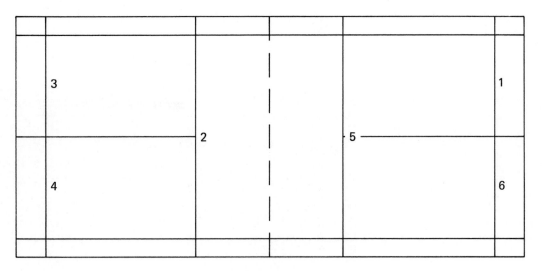

Figure 6.2
Clear-drop drill for six students

3. Students spread out and practice underhand strokes against the wall while the instructor circulates and makes corrections as needed.

LESSON 6: CROSSCOURT NET SHOTS

I. Preparation

A. Set up the courts.
B. Have rackets and shuttles available for early arrivals.

II. Content and Concepts

A. Physical Conditioning. Exercises can be led by the instructor or a student leader.
B. Review. Review net shots (Chapter 5, Lesson 14). After a brief review of hairpin net shots, students practice while instructor circulates and makes corrections as needed.
C. Crosscourt Net Shots. Using the chalkboard, the instructor defines and illustrates the crosscourt net shot.

   1. Crosscourt net shot travels parallel to the net cord from one side of the court to the other and crosses the net just as the shuttle loses force and falls on the opponent's side of the net; the shuttle should not rise more than 3 inches above the net. The flight pattern is:

   This shot must be played with care. It should be played when the opponent is in the back half of the court or well over to one side. It can also be played after the opponent has played a hairpin, but the shot must cross the net low enough so that the shuttle descends as soon as it crosses the net; the "touch" must be precise. This shot is easiest to make when the shuttle is met at or higher than net level, thus the need for getting to the shuttle as quickly as possible.

   2. The procedures for executing crosscourt net shots are as follows:

      a. Students arrange themselves on the court as shown in Figure 6.3, with the racket-side foot forward and the off-racket foot on or near the short service line.
      b. Put the shuttle in play with an underhand stroke, with the racket head not quite perpendicular to net. Both players then attempt to keep the shuttle in play with crosscourt net shots. Both racket grip and stroke should be firm.
      c. Stroke the shuttle so that it stays on the hitter's side of the net until just before it crosses, when it should then tick the net and fall in the alley.
      d. When the shuttle is tumbling, allow it to straighten out before hitting it; when the shuttle is not tumbling, take it as close to net level as possible, making the stroke easier.

D. Practice

   1. Students go to their courts and practice forehand crosscourt net shots while the instructor circulates and makes corrections as needed.

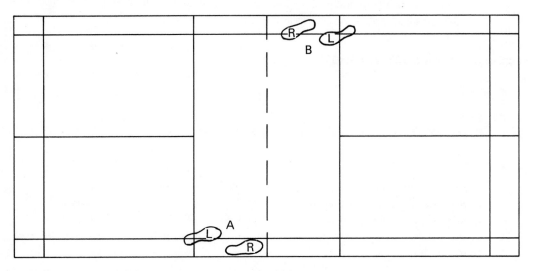

Figure 6.3
Students arranged on court for crosscourt practice

2. After a few minutes, students change alleys, keep same footwork position, and practice backhand crosscourt net shots.
3. Players not practicing crosscourt net shots should practice low services or strokes against the wall. After six minutes, students who were practicing crosscourt shots move to the walls to practice the low service or practice stroking against the wall while those who were practicing against the wall move to the court for crosscourt practice. This procedure is repeated until all students have practiced the crosscourt shot.
4. After they have practiced these drills for 12 to 15 minutes each, arrange students on the court as shown in Figure 6.4. Students can then stroke crosscourt or hairpin net shots.

E. Play. For the remainder of the class period, permit the class to play. An intermediate class should know the fundamentals of play.

LESSON 7: ROUND-THE-HEAD STROKE

I. Preparation

A. Set up the courts
B. Have rackets and shuttles available for early arrivals.

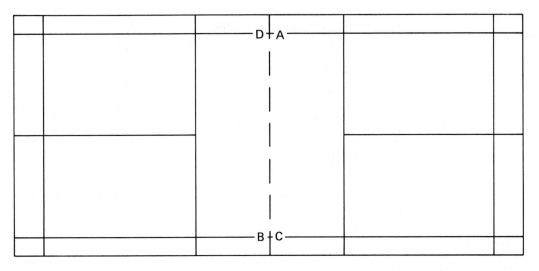

Figure 6.4
Students arranged on court for crosscourt and hairpin practice

II. Content and Concepts

A. Physical Conditioning. Exercises can be led by the instructor or a student leader.

B. Review. After a brief review of the clear, drop, and net shots, students can practice as the instructor circulates and makes corrections as needed.

C. The Round-the-Head Stroke. Using the chalkboard, the instructor defines and illustrates the round-the-head stroke.

    1. The round-the-head stroke is made with the forehand procedure when the shuttle is in the backhand position. It is hit with an overhead motion and the flight pattern of the shuttle depends on the shot, e.g., clear, drop, drive, or smash. This stroke is used to cover a weak backhand, to maintain an attacking position, and to serve as a strategic weapon.

    2. The procedures for executing the round-the-head shot are as follows:

        a. Assume the ready position.

        b. As the simulated shuttle approaches on the off-racket side of the body above the shoulder, bring the racket-side foot to a point behind the off-racket foot.

        c. Step toward the shuttle with the off-racket foot. This movement places the off-racket foot farther to the left than for a normal forehand.

        d. The racket is brought back in the normal fashion except that the forearm of the racket-side arm passes close to the top of the head as the racket is brought around in an arc, meeting the shuttle over the off-racket shoulder.

     e. Be sure that weight is on the left foot, the knees are bent, and the body is bent sideways and forward at the waist.

     f. Make contact with the racket head perpendicular to the shuttle.

     g. Remember that the angle of the racket head determines the flight of the shuttle.

  3. The round-the-head stroke is practiced as follows:

     a. Players arrange themselves on the court as shown in Figure 6.5.

     b. Players 1 and 3 serve the shuttle to players 2 and 4, who return it using the round-the-head stroke. After 10 strokes, players change positions.

     c. When all four players have hit 10 shots, they should try to keep the shuttle in play using round-the-head strokes.

     d. As students practice, the instructor circulates and makes positive corrections.

  D. Play. For the remainder of the class period, students play as the instructor rotates and corrects students as needed.

III. Teaching Techniques and Aids

  A. Emphasis is on good stroking (Figure 6.6). Important points to be observed are:

    1. Weight should be on the left foot.

    2. The body should be bent forward and to the left.

    3. The shuttle should be over the left shoulder.

    4. The palm of the hand should face forward when the stroke is made.

    5. The player should not overreach the shuttle. If he or she does overreach, weight and movement shift too much toward the sideline, making recovery difficult.

  B. Target areas at which the player directs shots can be placed on the floor.

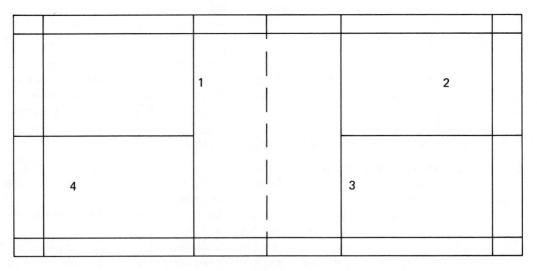

Figure 6.5
Students arranged on court for round-the-head practice

Figure 6.6
Correct body position for good stroking

LESSON 8: FOOTWORK

I. Preparation

   A. Set up the courts.
   B. Have rackets and shuttles ready for early arrivals.

II. Content and Concepts

   A. Physical Conditioning. Exercises can be led by the instructor or a student leader.
   B. Review

      1. Review the round-the-head stroke. Then students practice while the instructor circulates and makes corrections as needed.
      2. Review footwork drill (Chapter 5, Lesson 8). Then students can practice this drill on command while the instructor circulates and makes corrections as needed.
      3. Review the drive (Chapter 5, Lesson 13). After a brief review and demonstration of the drive, students practice while the instructor circulates and makes corrections as needed.

   C. Procedures for Practicing Sideline-to-Sideline Footwork and Drive

      1. Students arrange themselves on the court as shown in Figure 6.7.
      2. Student 1 puts the shuttle in play to student 2, who returns it to student 1 in the center

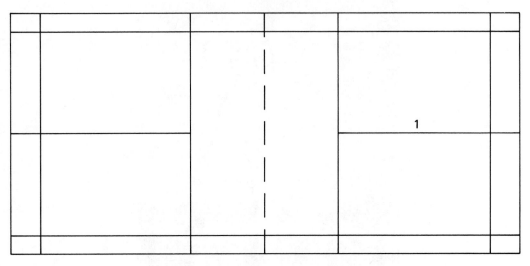

Figure 6.7
Students arranged on court for drive practice

position. Student 1 returns to student 2 approximately one step or so to either the forehand or the backhand. Student 2, using the appropriate footwork, returns to student 1. This process continues as student 1 gradually increases the angle until student 2 is moving the maximum distance across the court.

3. Student 2 always returns to home base after each shot.
4. Gradually pace (increase in shuttle speed) is also added to the shot, which increases the intensity of the drill.
5. After two to three minutes, students change positions.

III. Teaching Techniques and Aids

A. As skill increases, students can keep each other moving by driving down the line or cross-court.
B. Players can also use these drills to practice hitting drop shots off the forehand or backhand.
C. All of the preceding procedures are based on hitting with the stance closed on the forehand. Yet hitting with an open stance is also acceptable, indeed even recommended. Hitting with an open stance requires the following procedures (Figure 6.8):

  1. Take a short step with the racket-side foot in the direction of the sideline on the racket side of the body.
  2. Bring the off-racket foot to the racket-side foot using shuffle-type steps.

3. Continue moving toward the sideline with the racket-side foot. This places the racket-side foot near the sideline and the off-racket foot near the centerline.
4. To return to home base, push off with the racket-side foot using shuffle-type steps.

LESSON 9: THE DRIVE SERVE

I. Preparation

A. Set up target areas for low service.
B. Have rackets and shuttles available for early arrivals.

II. Content and Concepts

A. Physical Conditioning. Exercises can be led by the instructor or a student leader.
B. Review. After a brief review of the low service (Chapter 5, Lesson 7), students practice while the instructor circulates and makes corrections as needed.
C. The Drive Serve. Using the chalkboard, the instructor defines and illustrates the drive serve.

1. The drive serve is a flat shot directed toward the back of the opponent's court at the junction of the centerline and the doubles long service line in doubles or the singles long service line. The drive serve, used more often in doubles than in singles, is used sparingly and as a change of pace. The shuttle is aimed to a point just over the opponent's off-racket shoulder when served from the centerline; when served from the alley, the shuttle should not enter the correct court until the last minute (end of the flight path).

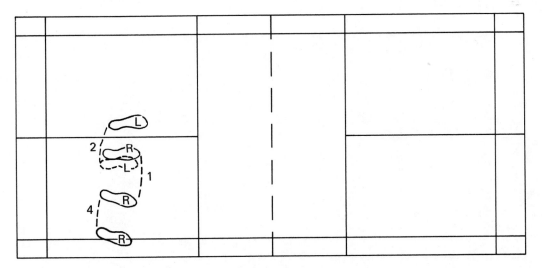

Figure 6.8
Alternate footwork for hitting with an open stance on the forehand

2. The procedures for executing the drive serve are as follows:

    a. Assume the position for executing the low service.

    b. Hold the shuttle by its base about shoulder high and opposite the racket-side arm.

    c. Using a modified grip, hold the racket-side arm back, with the wrist cocked and the racket head about shoulder high.

    d. As the shuttle is dropped, transfer weight to the front foot and bring the racket forward.

    e. Because contact with the shuttle must be made below the waist, hold the racket head down so that as contact is made the wrist is snapped forward, impelling the shuttle in a flat trajectory.

    f. To drive the serve, snap the wrist to give the racket head speed with which to drive the shuttle to the back line.

3. The procedures for practicing the drive serve are as follows:

    a. Students arrange themselves on the court as shown in Figure 6.9. Each has six shuttles.

    b. Students 1 and 3 practice the drive serve by serving to students 2 and 4. After six serves are made, students change positions.

    c. The instructor circulates and makes corrections as needed.

D. Play. Students play for the remainder of the class period.

III. Teaching Techniques and Aids

A. Using the target zones the instructor has made with strings, the student attempts to drive the shuttle between the string and net to the back, center corner.

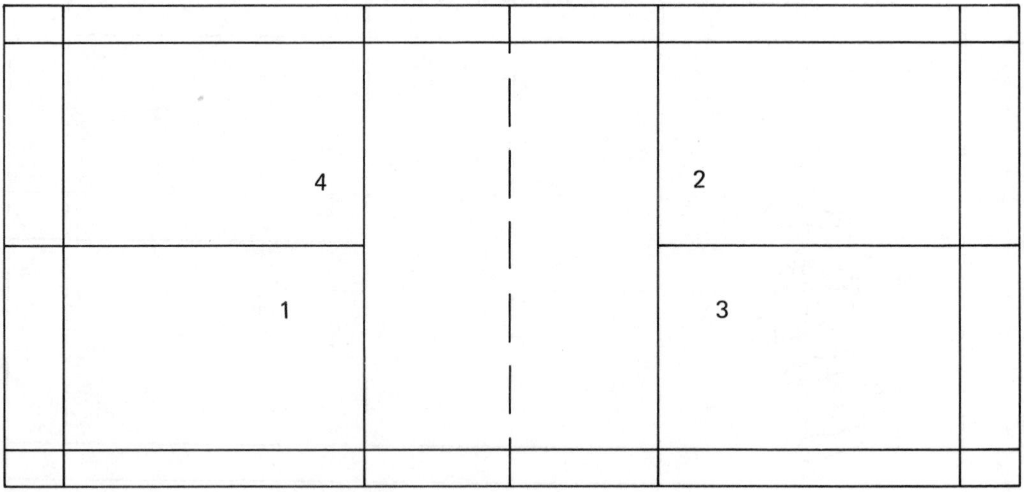

Figure 6.9
Students arranged on court for drive serve practice

B. By using less wrist action, the player can hit a low service. This gives the player two serves from the same base.

C. By delaying wrist movement, the player can keep opponents from jumping the serve.

LESSON 10: DOUBLES PLAY—COMBINATION SYSTEM

I. Preparation

A. Draw court diagrams on the chalkboard.

B. Set up the courts.

C. Have shuttles and rackets available for early arrivals.

II. Content and Concepts

A. Physical Conditioning. Exercises can be led by the instructor or a student leader.

B. Review

    1. Review the drive serve. Then students practice while the instructor circulates and makes corrections as needed.

    2. Review the systems of doubles play. Using the diagrams already drawn on the chalkboard, the instructor reviews the front-and-back and side-by-side systems of play. Then students play a five-minute game using both systems.

C. Doubles Play—Combination System

    1. Using the chalkboard, the instructor illustrates the combination system of doubles play. Emphasis is on the following points:

        a. The combination system is used in men's and women's doubles.

        b. Players stand side by side on defense.

        c. Players stand in a front-and-back position when on the attack (Figure 6.10).

        d. Players act as though they are rotating around an axis placed on the centerline a foot or two behind the short service line.

        e. Movement in one direction by a player produces movement in the opposite direction by the teammate.

        f. When a player on the attack clears, the teammate at the net moves back (directly back is best).

    2. The procedures for practicing the combination system of doubles play are as follows:

        a. Four players arrange themselves on each court as shown in Figure 6.11.

        b. Player 1 serves to player 3 and follows the serve to position ①.

        c. Player 3 plays a straight drop to position ⊗. Player 1 moves over to cover the shot and clears down the line. While player 1 moves over to play the shot, player 2 moves slightly to the right to position ② as shown. Then player 1, having cleared, drops straight back to midcourt while player 2 moves to the center of his or her court. Player 4 moves over to play the clear ④, while player 3 moves in to position ③.

        d. Each player plays in each position.

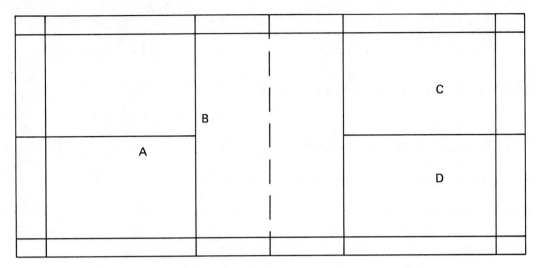

Figure 6.10
Court position for players on offense (A and B) and players on defense (C and D)

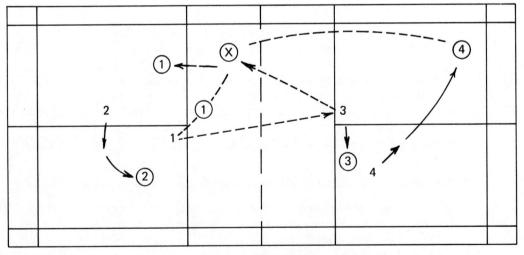

Key: --- path of shuttle
→ path of player

Figure 6.11
Students preparing to practice combination system

D. Play

    1. Students play for the remainder of the class period.

    2. The instructor circulates and assists students in understanding the procedures involved in the combination system of doubles play.

III. Teaching Techniques and Aids

A. In an instructional situation, different shot sequences can be developed and diagrammed on a chalkboard. Then players can walk through each sequence and practice the sequence while stroking the shuttle. Two objectives obtain: (1) Students must understand that they must perform the drills in order to learn the movement. (2) Each player must learn to stroke the shuttle to the proper place so that *it can be replayed.* Winning the point is not the intent.

B. During games played with these two objectives, the instructor stops play whenever necessary to explain how players should have moved in the preceding series of shots.

LESSON 11: THE FLICK SERVE

I. Preparation

A. Set up the courts.

B. Have rackets and shuttles available for early arrivals.

II. Content and Concepts

A. Physical Conditioning. Exercises can be led by the instructor or a student leader.

B. Review. After a brief review of the combination system and the related concepts, students play a five-minute game while the instructor circulates and makes corrections as needed.

C. The Flick Serve. Using the chalkboard, the instructor defines and illustrates the flick serve.

    1. The flick serve is delivered by a quick snap of the wrist just before contact with the shuttle. The flight pattern is:

The serve should land close to the baseline. The flick serve is directed just over the opponent's outstretched racket and is used as a change of pace, when the opponent rushes the serve, or when the opponent has difficulty retreating or has a weak overhead.

    2. The procedures for executing the flick serve are as follows:

        a. Assume the low service position.

        b. Hold the shuttle as it is held for the low service and the racket back at a height even with the shuttle; cock the wrist.

        c. Drop the shuttle and bring the racket forward.

        d. Immediately prior to contact, quickly snap the wrist to speed up the racket head. This extra speed places the racket head in a position to direct the shuttle upward.

        e. Aim shuttle to land on or just short of the long service line for doubles.

        f. Up to the point of impact, maintain the same motion as that for the low service.

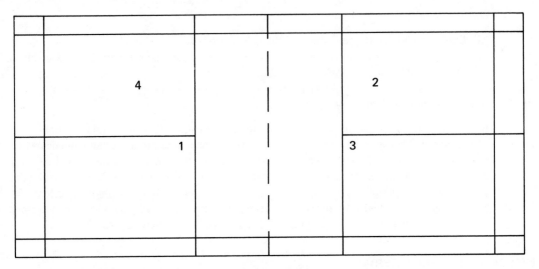

Figure 6.12
Students organized on court for flick serve practice

   3. The procedures for practicing the flick serve are as follows:

      a. Students arrange themselves on the court as shown in Figure 6.12.
      b. Students 1 and 3 serve to students 2 and 4 who are standing approximately 5 feet behind the short service line, with their racket held above their head.
      c. The server attempts to serve the shuttle just over the opponents' rackets to the designated area. After six serves, students rotate positions.
      d. As students practice, the instructor circulates and makes positive corrections as needed.

  D. Play. For the remainder of the class period, students play while the instructor circulates and makes corrections as needed.

LESSON 12: THE PUSH SHOT

I. Preparation

  A. Set up the courts.
  B. Have rackets and shuttles available for early arrivals.

II. Content and Concepts

  A. Physical Conditioning. Exercises can be led by the instructor or a student leader.
  B. Review. After a brief review of the flick serve, students practice while the instructor circulates, making corrections as needed.

C. The Push Shot. Using the chalkboard, the instructor defines and illustrates the push shot.

    1. The push shot, used to reply to a low service, directs the shuttle toward the sidelines just beyond the forecourt player and just in front of the backcourt player or directly at the opponent. The player should meet the shuttle at or above net level so that the flight path is downward, thus forcing the opponent to hit the shuttle upward.

    2. The procedures for executing the push shot are as follows:

        a. Assume a ready position.
        b. As the serve is made and the shuttle approaches, step forward with the racket-side foot and "push" the shuttle to either sideline. The shuttle can also be pushed directly at the opponent (Figure 6.13).
        c. Maintain regular grip, with the wrist cocked and held stationary.
        d. Make the stroke by straightening the arm as the shuttle is pushed toward the target.

    3. The procedures for practicing the push shot are as follows:

        a. Students arrange themselves on the court as they would for low service practice (Chapter 5, Lesson 7).
        b. Student 1 serves to student 2, who pushes the shot back either toward the server or toward the sidelines.
        c. After six serves, students exchange roles.

D. Play.

    1. Students are paired for play.
    2. The instructor circulates during play and makes corrections as needed.

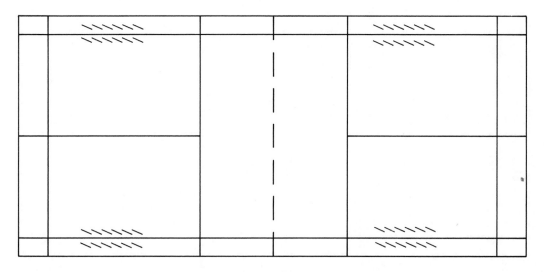

Figure 6.13
Court showing target areas for push shot

LESSON 13: SERVING

I. Preparation

    A. Set up the courts.

    B. Have rackets and shuttles available for early arrivals.

II. Content and Concepts

    A. Physical Conditioning. Exercises can be led by the instructor or a student leader.

    B. Review. After a brief review of the push shot, students practice as the instructor circulates, making corrections as needed.

    C. Service and Replying to Serves

        1. Students need the opportunity to practice serving and replying to serves in a simulated game situation. There are two important objectives:

            a. The server should attempt to serve so that the opponent cannot make an offensive reply.

            b. The receiver should attempt to make each reply an offensive shot.

        2. The procedures for practicing serving and replying to serves are as follows:

            a. Students arrange themselves on the court as shown in Figure 6.14.

            b. Students 1 and 3 serve to 2 and 4 with the assumption that each serve is the first of a game or an inning or following a point.

            c. Students 2 and 4 return the serve with the most appropriate reply.

            d. The instructor circulates and makes corrections.

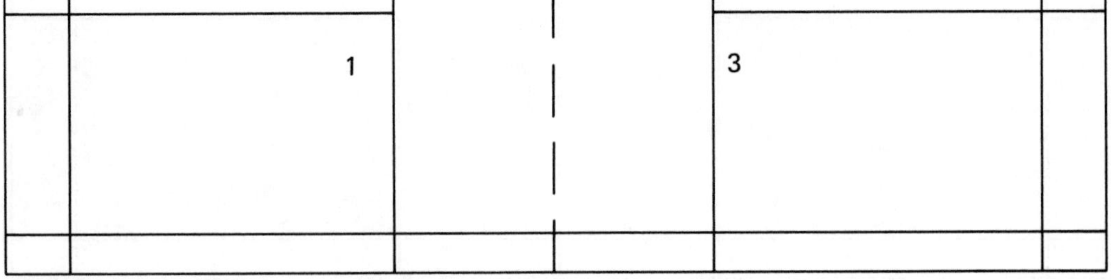

Figure 6.14
Students arranged on court for serving and replying practice

D. Play

1. Students are assigned partners and opponents.
2. Again, this play is designed for practice, not to win points.
3. The instructor circulates, corrects errors, and looks for common errors that can be discussed with the whole class later.

III. **Teaching Techniques and Aids**

To help students trying to develop accuracy in returning serves, the instructor should mark out target areas as shown in Figure 6.15.

LESSONS 14 THROUGH 17: PLAY

I. **Preparation**

A. Set up the courts.
B. Have rackets and shuttles available for early arrivals.

II. **Content and Concepts**

A. Physical Conditioning. Exercises can be led by the instructor or a student leader.
B. Play

1. Arrange doubles teams according to the schedule discussed in Appendix B.
2. As teams play, circulate, make corrections, and explain strategy.
3. While circulating, begin a systematic evaluation of students.

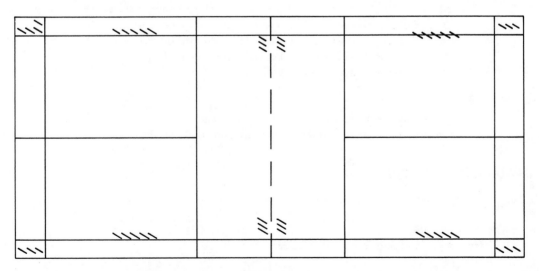

Figure 6.15
Court showing target areas for accuracy practice in replying to serves

LESSON 18: THE BACKHAND SMASH

I. Preparation

A. Set up the courts.
B. Have rackets and shuttles available for early arrivals.

II. Content and Concepts

A. Physical Conditioning. Exercise can be led by the instructor or a student leader.
B. Review. Review the backhand clear (Chapter 5, Lesson 5). Then students practice while the instructor circulates and makes corrections as needed.
C. The Backhand Smash

    1. The backhand smash begins as any other backhand overhead stroke but contact with the shuttle is made in front of the racket-side shoulder with the arm at approximately a 45-degree angle. The exact angle depends on the player's court position.
    2. The procedures for executing the backhand smash are as follows:

        a. From the ready position, pivot to a backhand hitting position.
        b. Bring racket back and point the elbow up toward the shuttle.
        c. As the shuttle approaches, transfer weight to the front foot.
        d. Begin to bring the arm forward vigorously as it outwardly rotates.
        e. Make contact with the shuttle in front, to the side, and forward, with the racket head perpendicular to the shuttle directing the shuttle downward at an angle.

    3. The procedures for practicing the backhand smash are as follows:

        a. Students arrange themselves on the court as shown in Figure 6.16.
        b. Students 1 and 4 serve to students 2 and 3, who attempt to smash the shuttle with a backhand. (At this point, form and technique are emphasized rather than power. As players gain confidence, more power can be put into the stroke.)
        c. The instructor circulates and makes corrections as needed.
        d. After six serves, students rotate positions.

D. Play

    1. Play continues as scheduled during the previous class period.
    2. The instructor circulates, makes corrections, and continues the evaluation process.

LESSON 19: THE STAR DRILL

I. Preparation

A. Set up the courts.
B. Have rackets and shuttles available for early arrivals.

II. Content and Concepts

A. Physical Conditioning. Exercises can be led by the instructor or a student leader.

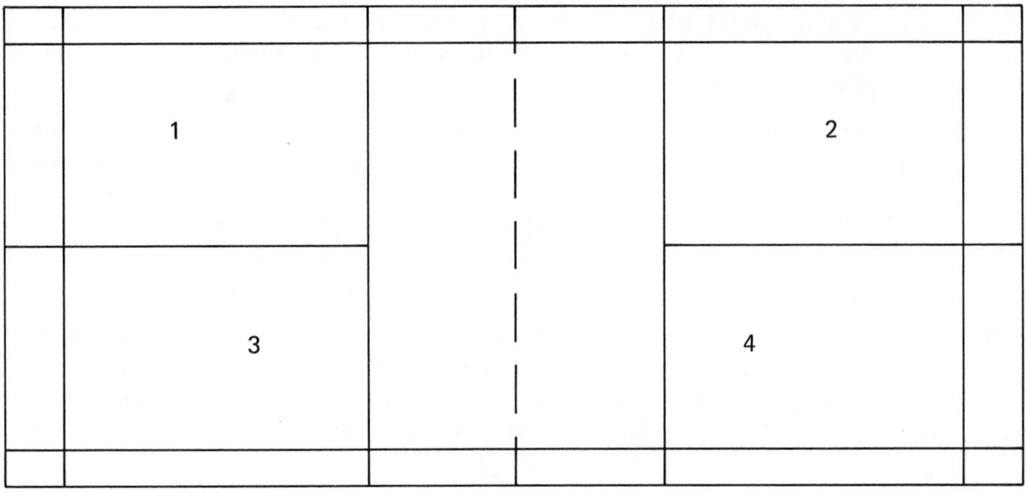

Figure 6.16
Students arranged on court for backhand smash practice

B. Review

1. Review the backhand smash. Then students practice while instructor circulates and makes corrections as needed.
2. Review star footwork drill (Chapter 5, Lesson 8). Then students practice while the instructor circulates and makes corrections as needed.

III. Teaching Techniques and Aids

A. The star drill involves three sequences to be taught after students learn the basic pattern.

1. In the first sequence, player 1, standing in the center of his or her court, hits the shuttle to player 2. Player 1 calls "One" and hits to point 1. Player 2 moves to point 1 and returns the shuttle to player 1 and returns to center court or home base. Player 1 calls "Two" and hits the shuttle to point 2. Player 2 moves to point 2 and hits the shuttle back to player 1 and moves back to home base. Player 1 calls "Three" and hits the shuttle to point 3. Player 2 moves to point 3 and hits the shuttle back to player 1 and moves back to home base. Player 1 calls "Four" and hits the shuttle to point 4. Player 2 moves to point 4 and hits the shuttle back to player 1 and moves back to home base. (See figures in parentheses in Figure 5.26 for the position of the four points.)

    a. When first learning this sequence, a player should not complete more than three sequences at a time.
    b. A player should not anticipate. Therefore, each time a player hits the shuttle back, he or she returns to the home base and awaits the next shot.

   c. Even though players in an actual game may need to move directly from one point to another, students learning this sequence should not be permitted to move from one point to another.

  2. In the second sequence, the same basic pattern is used except that player 1 does not call the numbers in sequence. The player can call numbers in any sequence but one to three or two to four.

  3. The third sequence has player 1 hitting the shuttle to player 2 without calling numbers. Player 2 must perceive the stroke, its force, and the shuttle's flight path and move in the appropriate direction, make the reply, and move back to home base.

B. The star drill can be used with player 1 standing in different locations. In this way students can practice hitting to different court areas under a measure of stress.

C. While one group of students is on the court practicing this drill, the remainder of the class should practice other skills around the perimeter of the court.

LESSON 20: PLAY

I. Preparation

A. Set up the courts.

B. Have rackets and shuttles available for early arrivals.

II. Content and Concepts

A. Physical Conditioning. Exercises can be led by the instructor or a student leader.

B. Review

  1. Review the star footwork drill. Then students practice while the instructor circulates and makes corrections as needed.

  2. Review singles serve (Chapter 5, Lesson 4). Then students practice while the instructor circulates and makes corrections as needed.

C. Play

  1. Students are paired and play a time-limited game of singles. The instructor circulates and makes positive corrections as needed.

  2. Doubles play continues as scheduled.

LESSON 21: CLEAR-DROP DRILL

I. Preparation

A. Set up the courts.

B. Have rackets and shuttles available for early arrivals.

II. Content and Concepts

A. Physical Conditioning. Exercises can be led by the instructor or a student leader.

B.   Review. After a brief review of the clear-drop drill, players practice while the instructor circulates and makes corrections as needed.
C.   Procedures for Practicing Clear-Drop Drill

   1. The clear-drop drill enables students to practice the forward-backward movement.

     a. Students arrange themselves as shown in Figure 6.17.
     b. Students 1 and 3 put the shuttle in play to students 2 and 4.
     c. Students 2 and 4 reply with either a clear or a drop to students 1 and 3, who use either shot as a reply.
     d. Both students mix up their replies so that each is forced to move from the backcourt to the forecourt and back again.

   2. Net shots can be added to this drill. They force the player to stay at the net until the shuttle is cleared. Moving too soon lets the opponent play another net shot to which the player cannot respond.

D.   Strategy. The following points should be stressed before students begin singles play:

   1. Singles strategy is designed to move the opponent out of the control position in center court.
   2. The bases of good strategy are:

     a. Serves of appropriate length
     b. Clears
     c. Tight drops
     d. Net shots

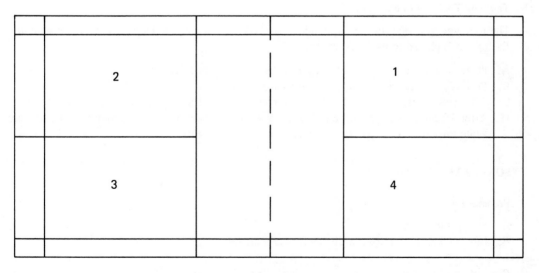

Figure 6.17
Students arranged on court for clear-drop drills

3. The smash is used only when its success is assured.
4. The player must move back to home base after the shot rather than waiting to see how the opponent will reply or how well the shot succeeded.
5. The player should change pace, shot trajectories, or whatever else to alter the pattern of play.
6. In serving and returning, the player must consider and reduce the angles of return. For example, in singles, he or she can serve to the corners adjacent to the centerline at the singles long service line.
7. The home base is in the center of the court but moves to either side or forward depending on the player's shot. The following points should be kept in mind:

   a. If the player hits to the deep forehand, he or she shades to the left.
   b. If the player hits to the deep backhand, he or she shades to the right.
   c. If the player hits a drop shot, he or she shades forward a bit.

8. When the player cannot get back to home base before the opponent strikes the shuttle, he or she should stop immediately and play from that location.

E. Play

1. Students are paired to play a singles game.
2. The instructor circulates and corrects errors. When students make tactical errors, the instructor should, at the conclusion of a rally, stop play and help them understand how the point could have been played more advantageously.
3. Students not playing can practice the low service on the perimeters of the court, use the wall for practice, or just hit together as possible. When the game in progress is completed, they take the court while those who just played practice.

III. Teaching Techniques and Aids

The following practice routine is valuable for students because the *emphasis is not on winning.* Each point is played to its fullest extent.

A. Player 1 serves to player 2. Player 2 returns with any shot desired.
B. Both play the remainder of the point as if they were in a game.
C. After this point is completed, player 2 serves to player 1 and the process continues.
D. After 10 points have been played, players who have been practicing around the court play while those who have played move off the court and practice.

LESSONS 22 THROUGH 27: PLAY

I. Preparation

A. Set up the courts.
B. Have rackets and shuttles available for early arrivals.

II. Content and Concepts

A. Physical Conditioning. Exercises can be led by the instructor or a student leader.

B. Play

    1. Opponents are assigned according to the schedule discussed in Appendix **B**.

    2. Each pair plays a regular singles game.

    3. The instructor circulates, makes corrections, and continues the evaluation process. The results should be shared with each student individually so that he or she knows what areas of the game need improvement.

LESSON 28: LOW SERVICE TEST

I. Preparation

A. Set up the courts for the low service test.

B. Prepare forms for recording test scores.

C. Prepare a double elimination tournament for singles, doubles, and, if possible, mixed doubles. The tournament bracket can be set up based on random pairings (see Appendix B) or an evaluation of players' skills during previous classes.

II. Content and Concepts

A. The low service test is given to the lower half of the tournament bracket first.

B. The upper half of the bracket starts the tournament.

C. When the lower half of the bracket has completed the test, the upper half takes the low service test and the lower half proceeds with the tournament.

D. All equipment is stored at tournament's end.

LESSON 29: CLEAR TEST

I. Preparation

A. Set up the courts for the clear test.

B. Prepare forms for recording test scores.

II. Content and Concepts

A. The clear test is given following the same procedure used in Lesson 27.

B. Tournament play continues.

C. All equipment is stored at tournament's end.

LESSON 30: WRITTEN EXAMINATION

I. Preparation

A. Arrange for a classroom in which to administer final examination.

B. Prepare the final written examination.

C. Prepare an evaluation form for students so that they can evaluate the class.

II. Content and Concepts

    A. The final written examination is administered.

    B. Students complete the class evaluation form.

7

Teaching Advanced Badminton

Beginning instruction is organized to give the student a fundamental knowledge of badminton and a good base for the execution of strokes. Competition or play at this level is designed to give the student a competitive and instructive experience. Winning is not the intent of the competition. Intermediate classes are designed to review fundamentals, increase skills, and increase stroke repertoire. Advanced instruction is designed to give the student practice in hitting advanced level strokes, modify stroke production for the purpose of deception, improve skills, and increase competitive competence.

To prepare adequately for instruction at this level, the instructor does a preliminary evaluation of each student. The evaluation chart discussed in Chapter 8 as well as the low service and clear tests can be used for this evaluation. Students should be assigned a partner with equal or better playing skills. Basic to this position is the premise that improvement is possible when a player is paired with another of equal or slightly better ability.

During advanced training, the student should be given the opportunity to learn officiating and to officiate class matches. A natural outcome of this instruction is a group of students who can act as officials for intramural matches and for local tournaments. Students in advanced classes should be encouraged to enter as many tournaments as feasible. Obviously, this depends on available funds, geographic location, and numerous other factors.

This chapter is similar in format to Chapters 5 and 6, with modifications noted as appropriate.

LESSON 1: ORIENTATION

I. Preparation

   A. Prepare handouts and samples of equipment.
   B. Prepare evaluation forms (see Table 8.1).

II. Content and Concepts

   A. Physical Conditioning. Exercises can be conducted by the instructor or a student leader.
   B. Introduction and Orientation to Course

C. Student Evaluation

1. Have students hit with each other.
2. Begin to evaluate students so that they can be paired to play in class.

LESSON 2: LOW SERVICE TEST

I. Preparation

A. Prepare the courts for the low service test.
B. Prepare forms for recording test scores.

II. Content and Concepts

A. Physical Conditioning. Exercises can be led by the instructor or a student leader.
B. Administration of Low Service Test
C. Student Evaluation

LESSON 3: CLEAR TEST

I. Preparation

A. Prepare the courts for the clear test.
B. Prepare forms for recording test scores.

II. Content and Concepts

A. Physical Conditioning. Exercises can be led by the instructor or a student leader.
B. Administration of Clear Test
C. Student Evaluation

LESSON 4: THE BACKHAND SERVE

I. Preparation

A. Prepare the courts for the low service test.
B. Prepare court assignments for students based on test results and evaluation.

II. Content and Concepts

A. Physical Conditioning. Exercises can be led by the instructor or a student leader.
B. Review

1. Review the low service (Chapter 5, Lesson 7). Then students practice while the instructor circulates and makes corrections as needed.
2. Review the drive serve (Chapter 6, Lesson 9). Then students practice while the instructor circulates and makes positive corrections as needed.

3. Review the flick serve (Chapter 6, Lesson 11). Then students practice while the instructor circulates and makes corrections as needed.

C. The Backhand Serve. Using the chalkboard, the instructor defines and illustrates the backhand serve.

1. The backhand serve is hit with a backhand stroke. The shuttle flies close to the net cord and lands in the front, center corner of the service court diagonally opposite. This serve takes less time to cross the net than others because it is hit in front of the body, is flatter and less susceptible to being smashed because it is hit just below waist level, and is more difficult to see because it is hit from a background of white clothes. The backhand serve is easier to hit than a flick serve. It also facilitates deception.

2. The procedures for executing the backhand serve are as follows:

a. Assume a stance just behind the short service line, with the racket-side foot slightly ahead of the off-racket foot.
b. Use the backhand grip but choke up on the racket handle for better control.
c. Hold the shuttle by the thumb and index finger, with its base at the center of the racket head and its skirt pointed toward the opposite court.
d. Hold the racket head below the hand and contact the shuttle below waist level.
e. As the fingers open and release the shuttle, bring the racket forward to strike it.
f. Direct the shuttle between the net cord and the first string for the low service.
g. Also try the "flick" serve from this position.

3. The procedures for practicing the backhand serve are as follows:

a. Students arrange themselves on the court as they would for a low service (Chapter 5, Lesson 7).
b. Students practice the backhand serve while the instructor circulates and makes corrections in a positive manner.

D. Play

1. Pair students and have them play doubles for the remainder of the class period.
2. Circulate and correct students as necessary regarding technique and strategy.

III. Teaching Techniques and Aids

A. The instructor can put a box in each corner of the court to serve as targets.
B. Some students may prefer to stroke the backhand serve from a position in which the toes are parallel rather than having the off-racket foot forward. This is strictly a matter of individual style.

LESSON 5: THE FAST DROP

I. Preparation

A. Set up the courts.
B. Have rackets and shuttles available for early arrivals.

II. Content and Concepts

A. Physical Conditioning. Exercises can be led by the instructor or a student leader.
B. Review

    1. Review the clear (Chapter 5, Lesson 5). Then students practice while the instructor circulates and makes corrections as needed.
    2. Review the drop (Chapter 5, Lesson 6). Then students practice while the instructor circulates and makes necessary corrections.
    3. Review the backhand serve. Then students practice while the instructor circulates and makes corrections as needed.

C. The Fast Drop. Using the chalkboard the instructor defines and illustrates the fast drop.

    1. The fast drop is a shot that has a straighter flight pattern than the regular drop; thus, it crosses the net close to the cord and carries out farther into the court as it passes into the opponent's court. It is used to put the shuttle on the floor as soon as possible or when a slow drop might be smashed. It also serves as a change of pace. The fast drop is executed in exactly the same way as the regular drop except for the angle and racket head speed.
    2. The procedures for executing the fast drop are as follows:

        a. Use the steps listed in Chapter 5, Lesson 6.
        b. Increase the racket head speed so that the shuttle descends more rapidly.

    3. The procedures for practicing the fast drop are as follows:

        a. Students arrange themselves on the court as shown in Figure 7.1.

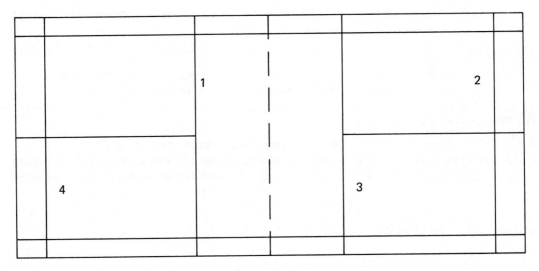

Figure 7.1
Students arranged on court for fast drop practice

      b. Student 1 serves to student 2, who attempts a fast drop.

      c. After six attempts, students change positions.

      d. The instructor circulates and makes corrections as needed. The following points should be emphasized:

          (1) The racket head must be over the shuttle.

          (2) The racket head should be square or perpendicular to the shuttle.

          (3) The shuttle should cross the net as close to the cord as possible.

          (4) By changing the speed of the racket head, the pace of the shuttle can be altered. This can be of help strategically.

D. Play

    1. For the remainder of the class period, students play as they are arranged on the court for practice.

    2. The instructor circulates and makes corrections as needed.

LESSON 6: THE HALF-PACED SMASH

I. Preparation

A. Set up the courts.

B. Have rackets and shuttles available for early arrivals.

II. Content and Concepts

A. Physical Conditioning. Exercises can be led by the instructor or a student leader.

B. Review

    1. Review the fast drop. Then students practice while the instructor circulates and makes corrections as needed.

    2. Review the smash (Chapter 5, Lesson 12). Then students practice while the instructor circulates and makes corrections as needed.

C. The Half-Paced Smash. Using the chalkboard, the instructor defines and illustrates the half-paced smash.

    1. The half-paced smash is executed like any other smash but with the racket face slightly open at contact with the shuttle, thereby giving it less pace. It is used more often in singles and mixed doubles than in doubles. Used to place the shuttle at midcourt on the open sides, the half-paced smash serves more as a placement shot than a power shot. The stroke for the half-paced smash is exactly the same as that for the smash except that immediately prior to contact with the shuttle the racket face is open which gives less pace and adds deception.

    2. The procedures for executing the half-paced smash are as follows:

      a. Use the procedures for executing the smash (Chapter 5, Lesson 12).

b. Proceed exactly as directed except that just before contact with the shuttle, open the racket face, i.e.:

or close it, i.e.:

directing the shuttle in the direction of the arrows.

3. The procedures for practicing the half-paced smash are as follows:

a. Students arrange themselves as shown in Figure 7.2.
b. Student 1 serves to student 2, who attempts to hit a half-paced smash.
c. The instructor circulates and makes corrections.
d. After six serves, students change positions.

D. Play. The instructor arranges students for play (singles or doubles) according to the schedule discussed in Appendix B.

LESSON 7: THE BRUSH SHOT

I. Preparation

A. Set up the courts.
B. Have rackets and shuttles available for early arrivals.

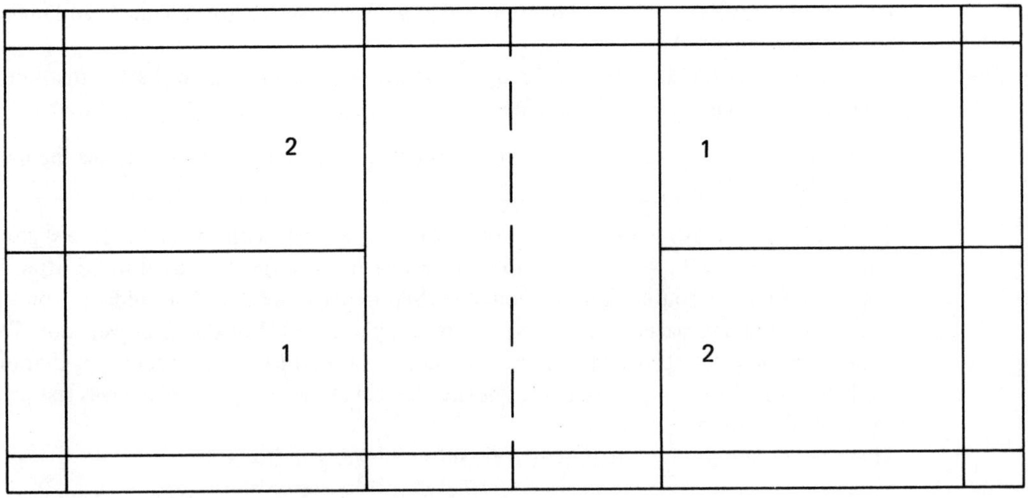

Figure 7.2
Students arranged on court for half-paced smash practice

II. Content and Concepts

A. Physical Conditioning. Exercises can be led by the instructor or a student leader.

B. Review

1. Review the half-paced smash. Then students practice while the instructor circulates and makes corrections as needed.
2. Review net shots (Chapter 5, Lesson 14). Then students practice while the instructor circulates and makes positive corrections.

C. The Brush Shot. Using the chalkboard, the instructor defines and illustrates the brush shot.

1. The brush shot is a shot used when the shuttle crosses just above and close to the net and a regular stroke might cause the player to hit the net. It is made by cutting across the shuttle by swinging the racket from the racket side of the body in a direction parallel to the net; the forehand face makes contact with the shuttle. Even though the swing is hard, the slicing action of the racket keeps the shuttle in the court.
2. The procedures for executing the brush shot are as follows:

   a. From the ready position, take a step in the direction of the net with the racket-side foot.
   b. At the same time, swing the racket, with the head of the racket above and parallel to the net cord, from the racket side of the body toward the off-racket side.
   c. Strike the shuttle midway through the arc.

3. The procedures for practicing the brush shot are as follows:

   a. Students arrange themselves as shown in Figure 7.3.
   b. Students 1 and 3 serve to students 2 and 4, attempting to pass the serve over the net approximately 3 feet above the net cord. As the shuttle crosses the net, students 2 and 4 attempt to return the shuttle with a brush shot.
   c. After several serves, students change procedures.

      (1) Have students in pairs practicing net shots.
      (2) Whenever a shuttle is above the net, the opposing player should attempt to return the shuttle with a brush shot.

LESSON 8: OFFICIALS AND OFFICIATING

I. Preparation

A. Set up the courts.
B. Have rackets and shuttles available for early arrivals.

II. Content and Concepts

A. Physical Conditioning. Exercises can be led by the instructor or a student leader.
B. Review. After a brief review of the half-paced smash, students practice while the instructor circulates and corrects errors.

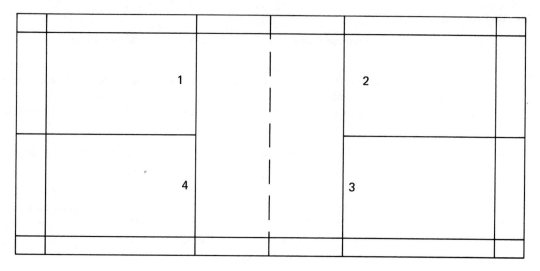

Figure 7.3
Students arranged on court for brush shot practice

C. Officials and Officiating

1. Officials start the match correctly, make sure that all players abide by the rules, eliminate the need for players to call their own game, and rule on all questions related to interpretations of the badminton rules.
2. Officials needed for the conduct of a match include a referee, umpire, service judge, and line judge.
3. The duties of the officials can be summarized as follows:

   a. The referee is responsible for the conduct of a tournament and resolves appeals from players relative to a point of interpretation.
   b. The umpire must know the badminton rules, makes sure that the court is ready for play, calls all scores clearly, prepares scorecards, and sees that line judges are properly placed. If a service judge is not available, the umpire is responsible for service faults; he or she also makes sure that there are a sufficient number of shuttles on hand, carries out the toss correctly, starts and concludes the match, and calls the server's score first.
   c. The service judge must see that the rules regarding service are not violated by the server or receiver. However, the umpire may also call service faults.
   d. The line judge should call all shuttles on his or her line. If the shuttle is out, he or she spreads both arms horizontally to one side and calls "out" loudly; if it is in, he or she does nothing.

D. Play

1. The instructor serves as a referee.
2. The instructor assigns players and officials according to the class size.
3. The instructor circulates and helps where necessary.

III. Teaching Techniques and Aids

A. From this point on, the instructor should assign competitive units based on the schedule discussed in Appendix B.

B. Each student serves as an umpire, a service judge, and a line judge.

C. The instructor should prepare a scorecard (Figure 7.4) that can be used for singles or doubles matches.

SCORECARD

Class _____   Player   Event _____

Court _____   _____ vs _____   Umpire _____

Date _____   _____ vs _____   Service Judge _____

Line Judge _____

Players

Doubles

Player A R L̷ 1̷2̷/345̷/ ✓

Player B R̷ L

Player C R L̷ 12̇345̷/ ✓

Player D R̷ L

Singles

Player E   123̇/   456789/

Player F   12345/   67/

Player G

Player H

Results: _____   Umpire's Signature _____

---

1. When a doubles match is played, cross out the appropriate letter to designate the player in the right or left court.
2. When the first server of team 1 (A) loses the serve, place a dot (˙) over the score since in doubles the team beginning the service only has one opportunity to serve. When player A loses the serve, the inning ends and should be marked by a slash (/).
3. From the second inning on, each member of the team has an opportunity to serve. Therefore, when the first server loses the serve, place a dot (˙) over the score; when the second server loses the serve, mark it with a checkmark (✓) and put the slash (/) at the end.
4. When the score is the same after the second server loses the serve as it was when the first server lost the serve, it should be marked (✓̇/).

Figure 7.4
Class scorecard

LESSON 9: STRATEGY

I. Preparation

    A. Set up the courts.

    B. Have rackets and shuttles available for early arrivals.

II. Content and Concepts

    A. Physical Conditioning. Exercises can be led by the instructor or a student leader.

    B. Strategy

        1. Table 7.1 describes basic situations and shot options.

        2. Using the chalkboard, the instructor should go over these situations with the entire class.

    C. Play

        1. Play continues as scheduled.

        2. The instructor circulates, corrects errors, and assists students as needed.

LESSONS 10 THROUGH 27: PLAY

During these 18 class periods, students compete against each other. Competitive units are assigned according to the schedule discussed in Appendix B. During these games, the instructor helps players to practice holding the shuttle, using body movements for deception, and varying the pace of the shuttle by changing the angle of the racket head upon contact. The instructor should evaluate students on how well they are performing the basic fundamentals of badminton. A single elimination tournament with a consolation bracket should complete the course.

LESSON 28: LOW SERVICE TEST

I. Preparation

    A. Set up the courts for the low service test.

    B. Prepare forms for recording test scores.

    C. Prepare a double elimination tournament for singles, doubles, and, if possible, mixed doubles. The tournament bracket can be set up based on random pairings (see Appendix B) or an evaluation of players' skills during previous classes.

II. Content and Concepts

    A. The low service test is administered to the lower half of the tournament bracket first.

    B. The upper half of the bracket begins the tournament.

    C. When the lower half of the bracket has completed the test, the upper half takes the low service test and the lower half proceeds with the tournament.

    D. All equipment is stored at tournament's end.

Table 7.1
Basic Situations and Stroke-Moves*

Situation	Shuttle Position	Stroke-Moves	Direction	Reason	Opponent's Possible Replies	Your Recovery
Rearcourt	High	Smash or sliced smash Fast drop shot Checked smash Attacking clear	Straight or center or cross-court Straight or cross-court Straight or center To corners or center	To hit the ground or force a lift To force a lift To cause opponent to scramble and play a weak return To catch opponent off-balance and force a weak reply	Block High clear Whip Net return, clear Smash Drop Clear	Move forwards toward the midcourt ready to attack the net return Move quickly into the midcourt attack position or defense position
	High	High defensive clear	To center	You have been caught off balance and need time to recover. You hit it to the center to reduce the angle and make defense easier	Smash Clear Drop	Walk calmly to the midcourt and take up a defensive stance
Midcourt	High	As for the rearcourt. Now you are nearer the net and have more chance of hitting a winning move				
	Low	Block to the smash Clear Whip Net return to fast drop shot	Straight or center or cross-court Cross-court Center or sides	To force opponent to lift To move opponent to rearcourt To give him less recovery time and get it past him To force a lift	Forecourt attack Smash, clear or drop Forecourt attack	Midcourt attack Midcourt defense Midcourt attack Midcourt attack
	Shoulder height	Drive	Straight or cross-court	To give less time To force a lift or a hasty stroke	Block, clear or drive	Midcourt attack position
Forecourt	Above net height	Smash Brush shot Dab Push	Downwards at or past opponent	To hit the ground or force a weak return To force a lift	Block or hit without control	Attack position on the edge of the forecourt
	Below net height	Jab, tumbler, or spinner Net whip	Straight or to the center Angled	To keep the shuttle close to the net and make it difficult to return To force a high clear to the midcourt To get the shuttle past the opponent and to force a weak return	Net return High lift Net whip Scramble and take late	Attack position on the edge of the forecourt Attack position in midcourt
	Low, near the ground	High defensive clear	Center	You have been caught off-balance and need time to recover. You hit the shuttle to the center to reduce the angle and make defense easier	Smash Clear Drop shot	Walk calmly to the midcourt and take up a defensive stance

*Reprinted from Jake Downey. "An Analysis of the Game." *Badminton USA* 39 (November 1979): 8. Used by permission.

LESSON 29: CLEAR TEST

I. Preparation

    A. Set up the courts for the clear test.

    B. Prepare forms for recording test scores.

II. Content and Concepts

    A. The clear test is given according to the procedures used in Lesson 28.

    B. Tournament play continues.

    C. All equipment is stored at tournament's end.

LESSON 30: WRITTEN EXAMINATION

I. Preparation

    A. Arrange for a classroom in which to administer final examination.

    B. Prepare the final written examination.

    C. Prepare an evaluation form for students so that they can evaluate the class.

II. Content and Concepts

    A. The final written examination is given.

    B. Students complete the class evaluation form.

8

Student Evaluation

Students want to know if they are making progress. While each player has an idea about his or her skill level, objective evidence of success strongly motivates him or her to continue practicing. Appropriate skill and knowledge tests accurately assess a player's badminton ability. Subjective appraisals of performance based on movement models provide a guide for correcting stroke procedures and movement patterns. Each time a student performs well the instructor should say so, thus reinforcing the stroke or movement pattern.

Evaluation is not just a terminal activity. Rather, it should be (1) continuous, (2) related to course objectives—affective, cognitive, and psychomotor, and (3) consist of activity-related skills. The latter point is significant even though skill evaluation is a static process rather than a part of a dynamic game.

SUBJECTIVE SKILLS EVALUATION

Top level performance in badminton requires that all required movements be executed in proper sequence and that the player be in proper position for stroke execution. The purpose of evaluation by the instructor is to analyze for the player, until such time as the player can complete an adequate self-assessment of personal skills, the areas of performance conforming to accepted standards and those requiring additional work. An evaluation form such as that shown in Figure 8.1 gives an instructor a basis for the evaluation.

Each student should be evaluated often by the instructor on every element in Figure 8.1 using the symbols given in the key. If the more recent rating is better than the preceding one, the earlier rating is crossed out, e.g., S. O. When the student falls short of accepted performance standards, the instructor should note the problem and correct it in a positive manner as soon as possible. The instructor can schedule times during which to make evaluations. Although daily evaluation is impossible in most classes, this writer believes that use of an evaluation form should be frequent to individualize instruction. Whenever an evaluation is done, the instructor should review the results with the student and demonstrate the correct techniques. Any part of the class period when the student is practicing or playing (before, during, or after class) can be used for evaluation. During the course, students will note progress because the rating should gradually approach the "usually" or "always" categories.

Figure 8.1
Evaluation of Student's Badminton Skills

Student Name	Ready Position: Feet spread about a shoulders' width apart	Ready Position: Weight on balls of feet	Ready Position: Knees slightly bent	Ready Position: Upper body inclined forward	Ready Position: Off-racket foot slightly ahead	Ready Position: Head up, with racket held out in front about head high	Ready Position: Pivots on appropriate foot	Stroking Position: Body perpendicular to net	Stroking Position: Weight on rear foot	Stroking Position: Racket cocked behind head	Stroking Position: Transfers body weight forward	Stroke Execution (General): Begins body rotation with hips	Stroke Execution (General): Extends arm as stroke is made	Stroke Execution (General): Pronates arm and flexes hand at wrist as racket head is driven *through* stroke	Stroke Execution (General): Always moves toward shuttle when stroking	Stroke Execution (General): Shows same basic position for all strokes until just prior to contact with shuttle	The Clear: Has good height (defensive)	The Clear: Has good length	The Clear: Has appropriate height (offensive)	The Clear: Is used strategically	The Drop: Lands close to net	The Drop: Passes over net close to net cords	The Drop: Is used strategically

Figure 8.1 *(continued)*

	The Smash					The Drive				Net Flight			The Serve							Play						
Student Name	Is hit hard	Is sharply angled	Is used in doubles whenever possible	Is used in singles when a point is possible	Is hit parallel to floor	Passes over net close to cord	Usually is hit down sidelines	Has good length	Is played when possible with racket at net level	Is tight to net cord	Is used strategically	In doubles, crosses net close to cord	Is usually served to center corners	Is usually low service	In singles, has good height	Has good depth	Is usually served to center of court	Is usually the high, deep serve	Maintains mobile position	Returns to home base after each shot in singles	Covers own court in doubles	Adjusts to partner's skills	Plays up and back on attack; side by side on defense	Does not overrun the shuttle	Mixes up serves	Does not let shuttle get behind body

Key: A = always; U = usually; O = occasionally; S = seldom; N = Never

Use of this evaluation form should not be limited to beginning badminton students. It can also serve as a preliminary evaluation of students in intermediate and advanced classes. Instructors in agencies or clubs can use the form during instructional periods. Finally, coaches can use it for team evaluation and scouting.

AFFECTIVE DOMAIN TESTS

Every instructor wants students to develop certain ideals, values, and attitudes. Testing for these is difficult. However, desirable or positive behavior can be noted by the instructor with a plus on the roll book; undesirable or negative behavior can be noted with a minus. If negative behavior occurs, the instructor should talk individually to each of the players involved about the appropriate behavior. Positive behavior should always be rewarded verbally.

COGNITIVE DOMAIN TESTS

Written examinations and formal and informal oral examinations evaluate the cognitive domain, i.e., the student's knowledge of the material covered in class. Although either objective or essay tests can be given, beginning teachers should perhaps give objective tests. Two or three short tests on specific subjects covered during the course are preferred to a comprehensive final. For example, a test on the rules of badminton could be given before students begin to play the game. This would enable the instructor to clear up such problems as fully understanding the procedures for setting when the score is tied, fully understanding service procedures, and knowing the ways in which the doubles service and playing courts differ from the singles service and playing courts. Later, students could be tested on terms, historical background, and strategy.

For beginning classes, approximately 10% of test questions should concern historical background; 10%, equipment; 30%, rules and techniques; and 50%, strategy. Tests for intermediate classes should focus 60% on strategy and 40% on rules and techniques. For advanced classes, strategy questions should represent 65% of the test; rules and techniques, 25%; and officiating, 10%. Advanced level tests should address tactical situations and playing options.

PSYCHOMOTOR DOMAIN TESTS

Psychomotor tests are yet another evaluation technique. Generally, but especially in beginning classes, because of time and emphasis, psychomotor tests are used to measure the student's ability to perform the low service and the clear.

I. **Low Service Test**

    A. Orientation. The low service has two very important components: (1) the shuttle should be descending and close to the net cord as it crosses the net; and (2) the length of the serve must be to the short service line. Most tests simply total the scores made at the net and on the floor as a measure of skill, as shown in Table 8.1.

           The low service test should be given at least twice during the instructional period—once toward the midpoint of the instruction, which serves as a basis for evaluating improvement, and again at the conclusion of the course as part of the final examination.

Table 8.1
Performance Standards for Low Service Test

Performance	Net	Floor	Total
Average	13-28	10-27	26-52
Good	25-35	22-34	49-65
Excellent	34-50	33-50	63-100

Performance standards should be developed by each instructor for each particular student population. Students should be able to perform at the levels shown in Table 8.2.

B. Procedures for Administering Brumbach Low Service Test (Modified)*

1. Equipment and Setup

   a. Figure 8.2 shows a diagram of a court prepared for the low service test.
   b. Twelve new shuttlecocks, one good racket, two pieces of light chalk (if needed to mark target zones and values), forms for recording test scores, and a chair or stool for holding shuttles are needed. (The chair should be placed so that the player can reach the shuttles without changing position or interfering with the stroke.)
   c. A cord is strung tightly 6 inches above and parallel to the net; another cord is strung 6 inches above and parallel to the first.

2. Test

   a. The student serves six shuttles from the right court into the diagonally opposite court and six shuttles from the left court into the diagonally opposite court.
   b. The student may serve from anywhere behind the restraining line.
   c. The serve must be legal and pass over the net to be officially scored.

3. Scoring

   a. A service passing between the net and the first cord is scored as 5 points; between the first and second cord, 3 points; over the top cord, 1 point.
   b. A service passing over the net and landing in the zone parallel to the short line is awarded 5 points; landing in one of the triangular zones, 4 points; landing in the first semicircular zone, 3 points; landing in the second semicircular zone, 2 points; landing anywhere else on the court, 1 point.
   c. The score for each service is the sum of the net and floor scores.
   d. The score is awarded according to the point where the base of the shuttle strikes the floor. Shuttles falling on a line are awarded the higher score.
   e. Illegal serves are not counted but can be re-served.
   f. A shuttle deflected by a cord is re-served if the instructor decides that the deflection negatively affected the score.
   g. The student's final score is the sum of the best of the six services from each court.

*Unpublished research conducted by Wayne B. Brumbach at the University of Oregon, Eugene, with students from the Service Course Division. Subsequent use by this writer resulted in modifications. Used by permission.

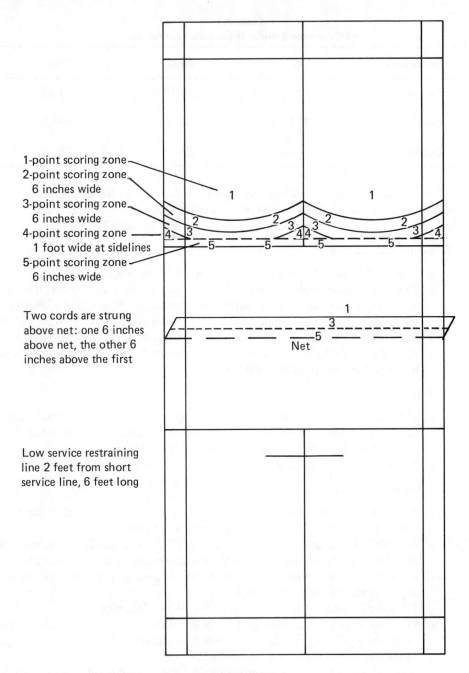

1-point scoring zone
2-point scoring zone
  6 inches wide
3-point scoring zone
  6 inches wide
4-point scoring zone
  1 foot wide at sidelines
5-point scoring zone
  6 inches wide

Two cords are strung
above net: one 6 inches
above net, the other 6
inches above the first

Low service restraining
line 2 feet from short
service line, 6 feet long

Figure 8.2
Court prepared for low service test

4. Additional personnel

   a. One student acts as a service judge.
   b. Two students, one at either end of the net, call *net* scores. One student calls *floor* scores.
   c. One student serves as a recorder.

5. Instructions to be read to students

   a. You are to be tested on your ability to perform the low service by attempting to serve six shuttles from each court over the net and into the appropriate target areas on the diagonally opposite court. Your score will be the sum of the best five services from each court.
   b. You may serve from anywhere behind the restraining line.
   c. You must serve the shuttles legally so that they pass over the net (instructor indicates the various zones and the corresponding score at this time) and land in the target areas on the floor (at this time instructor reviews the scoring on the floor).
   d. Every shuttle at which you swing counts as one of your 12 serves. Shuttlecocks failing to go over the net, going out of bounds, or falling short of the scoring zone will score no points. Shuttlecocks striking a cord and altering the flight will be re-served. Your scores at the net will be scored as follows:

   (1) Between net and first cord   5 points
   (2) Between first and second cord   3 points
   (3) Over the second cord   1 point

   Your scores on the floor will be scored as follows:

   (1) Six-inch zone behind short service line   5 points
   (2) Triangular zones in each corner   4 points
   (3) First semicircular zone   3 points
   (4) Second semicircular zone   2 points
   (5) Any serve landing in proper service court 1 point

C. Visual Interpretation of Results. Used in another fashion, the low service test has even more value as a measuring instrument. The scores can be analyzed visually, which gives the instructor an idea of the flight pattern. For example, look at the following scores:

		1	2	3	4	5	6	7	8	9	10	11	12	Totals	
Student A	Net	3	5	1/	3	5	5	1/	1	5	1	3	1	32	64
	Floor	4	3	/3	4	5	4	/3	3	0	3	3	3	32	
Student B	Net	0/	1	1	3	0	1	3	1	3/	3	1	3	17	58
	Floor	/0	5	5	5	0	3	4	4	/0	5	5	5	41	

Total scores are only 6 points apart. The score on the floor target is 9 points better for student B than student A; however, the crucial element is the net score. Student A served only 5 of the 12 shuttles above all lines, as indicated by the score of 1, each of which went into the first semicircular zone, as indicated by the score of 3. Student B served 5 shuttles over all lines (the score of 1), 5 over the first line (score of 3), while 2 went into the net (score of 0). Thus, it is noted that all the serves were either 6 inches or higher above the net or did not cross it. Student A's performance is much better (15 points) than that of student B because a serve passing close to the net is better than one passing high over the net. Student B will have to make more of an adjustment to become an excellent server.

II. Clear Test

A. Orientation. The second important skill in badminton is the ability to clear the shuttle high and deep to the opposite court. This ability consists of two important elements: (1) the ability to achieve good length (within 6 inches of the baseline) and (2) the ability to achieve sufficient height so that the hitter can recover the home base. The height of the shuttle depends on how much difficulty the player is having and how much recovery time he or she needs, i.e., whether the player is well out of position or attempting a very difficult return.

The clear test is designed for use by beginning, intermediate, and advanced players. Beginning players take a position at center court (*X*), whereas intermediate and advanced players begin in the box (Figure 8.3).

Like the low service test, the clear test should be given at least twice during the instructional period—once toward the midpoint of instruction to serve as a basis for evaluating improvement and again at the conclusion of the course to serve as a part of the final examination. Similarly, performance standards should be developed for each particular student population. Students should be able to perform at the levels shown in Table 8.2.

B. Procedures for Administering Brumbach Clear Test (Modified)*

1. Equipment and Setup

a. Figure 8.3 shows a court prepared for the clear test.

*Unpublished research conducted by Wayne B. Brumbach at the University of Oregon, Eugene, with students from the Service Course Division. Subsequent use by this writer resulted in modifications. Used by permission.

Table 8.2
Performance Standards for Clear Test

Performance	Scores
Average	3-21
Good	18-30
Excellent	29-50

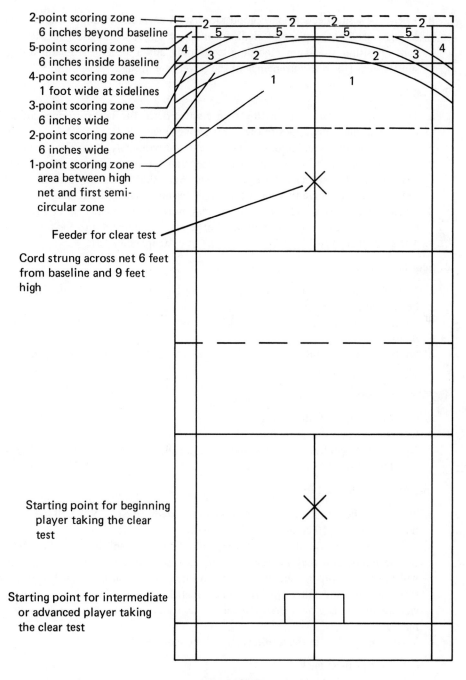

2-point scoring zone
6 inches beyond baseline

5-point scoring zone
6 inches inside baseline

4-point scoring zone
1 foot wide at sidelines

3-point scoring zone
6 inches wide

2-point scoring zone
6 inches wide

1-point scoring zone
area between high
net and first semi-
circular zone

Feeder for clear test

Cord strung across net 6 feet
from baseline and 9 feet
high

Starting point for beginning
player taking the clear
test

Starting point for intermediate
or advanced player taking
the clear test

Figure 8.3
Court prepared for clear test

   b. Twelve new shuttlecocks, two good rackets, an extra net strung across the court at a height of 9 feet, a piece of chalk for marking target scores and values and the student's position, forms for recording test scores, and a chair or stool for holding the shuttlecocks (for the convenience of the server) are needed.

2. Test

   a. The student is stationed on the *X* (beginner) or in the box (intermediate and advanced) on the court opposite the scoring zone (Figure 8.3).

   b. The server is positioned opposite the student approximately at the short service line.

   c. The server serves the shuttle in such a way that the student can hit it with an overhead stroke. The student attempts to clear every shuttle served. However, the server can rule out each serve that he or she feels does not result in a fair trial.

   d. When the serve is struck, the student may move as necessary. He or she attempts, using an overhead stroke, to send the shuttle over the net and into the target area.

   e. The student is given 12 attempts; only the best 10 are counted.

3. Scoring

   a. The shots are scored according to where the base of the shuttle lands. Shuttles landing on a line are awarded the higher value.

   b. Shuttles failing to clear the suspended net, hit out of bounds, or thrown receive no points.

   c. Shuttles touching the top of the suspended net and going over it are scored as other shots clearing the net.

4. Additional personnel

   a. One student records the scores.

   b. One student calls out the scores.

   c. One student watches the suspended net and calls "Short" for shuttles failing to pass over the net.

5. Instructions to be read to students

   a. You are to be tested on your ability to hit an overhead clear. You will have 12 shots, but only the best 10 count toward your score.

   b. You will stand in the designated area, and a high serve will be hit to you. When the shuttle is hit, you may move wherever you wish in order to make the stroke. You will attempt to hit the shuttle with an overhead stroke so that it will pass over the suspended net and fall within the zoned area. If, in the opinion of the server, a service hit to you is a poor one, the call of "No shot" will be made and another serve made.

   c. Your shots landing in the scoring area will be scored as follows:

     (1) Zone farthest back   5 points

     (2) Triangular zones in each corner   4 points

     (3) First semicircular zone   3 points

(4) Second semicircular zone   2 points
(5) Six-inch zone beyond the baseline   2 points
(6) Any shot clearing the net, falling in the court
     but not in one of the zones listed above   1 point

PHYSICAL FITNESS TESTS

Since physical fitness tests are given at the discretion of the instructor, the method of evaluation rests with the instructor. Most valuable, of course, would be drills and shuttle runs derived from badminton skills.

9

Coaching Badminton

Playing badminton well involves applying already learned skill and strategy fundamentals to a given tactical situation. Coaching, the process that enables the player to perform well, basically consists of overseeing the proper physical conditioning of players and improving individual performance to a point where all fundamentals become habitual. Both these essential elements in coaching are discussed in this chapter.

OVERSEEING PHYSICAL CONDITIONING

A coach recognizes that every player should maintain a good level of physical fitness at all times. When a player is in good condition, the specific conditioning programs related to badminton obtain results more quickly and he or she can perform at a better level sooner. Basically, the specific conditioning program has three phases: preseason, in-season, and postseason.

Preseason Conditioning

The preseason conditioning program should consist of rope jumping, stretching, weight training, and running. The fundamental purpose of this work is to develop agility, flexibility, strength, and cardiovascular efficiency. All this work can be done with or without racket work.

Rope jumping, either off both feet or alternating feet, helps players develop the capacity to maintain a bouncing motion on the court. In the beginning, players should jump rope for 15 to 30 seconds and gradually progress to 5 to 10 minutes and increase the pace of jumping. When prolonged, rope jumping helps develop cardiovascular endurance.

Stretching exercises are important because players must reach for the shuttle, bend the body to hit round-the-head strokes, and be able to reach and stretch to their body's limits without being injured. Two valuable exercises are the hurdle-stretch and the lunge.

The hurdle-stretch position (Figure 9.1) can be used to improve flexibility of the trunk and hips. In this position, the player sits on the floor and extends one leg forward and the other leg backward. The player then gradually reaches for the front foot, extending *without bouncing* until he or she can touch it. The player must alternate legs.

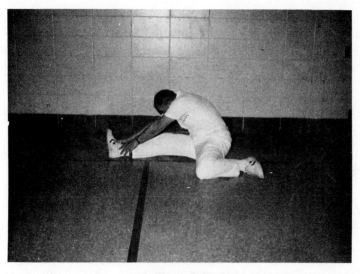

Figure 9.1
The hurdle-stretch

Another good stretching exercise is the lunge (Figure 5.27), which enables the player to stroke a shuttle at full reach (but not overextended) so that he or she can more easily return to home base. Further, it is better to reach for the shuttle than to overrun it and cramp the hitting position; the lunge keeps the player reaching and prevents overrunning. In this exercise, the student places the inside of one foot on the floor and extends the other foot forward. Again, this exercise is done gradually until the student's front lower leg is at right angles to the floor and to the thigh and the armpit of the same-side arm can be placed over the knee to get full extension.

Other flexibility exercises include the side bender, body twist, squat bender, and trunk twister. All beneficially affect the trunk, hips, and legs, and may be used for variety.

During the preseason, the player should engage in a weight training program that stresses both strength and endurance of the legs, arms, and shoulder girdles (more precisely the flexors of the hand at the wrist and the pronator and supinator muscles of the forearm). Strength and endurance are developed by increasing the weight used and the number of repetitions. If there is to be any emphasis, it should be on endurance. The particular type of weight training used (e.g., Universal TM machine, Nautilus TM, free weight, partner resistance) will depend on the facilities available.

Because start-and-stop movement is an integral part of competitive badminton, players should start a running program to increase cardiovascular conditioning during preseason. Alternating running and walking at first and then running and sprinting short distances should help the players' bodies adjust to the quick short dashes required in badminton. Shuttle runs utilizing the width of the court also can help players adjust to the needs of the game.

In-Season Conditioning

During the playing season, the preseason conditioning program should be tapered off so that most of the seasonal conditioning takes the form of drills and exercises related to badminton. One axiom in athletics is that all drills should evolve from the activity itself. Thus, the successful badminton coach uses those drills that improve the players' skills as well as condition their bodies.

Before going at an all-out pace, each player should warm up thoroughly—bending, stretching, practicing swinging as if he or she were actually playing the shots, and running short, easy sprints from side to side, from front to back, and diagonally on the court. Following individual warm up, players get on the courts and practice stroking at half speed. Gradually, stroking should be increased to full pace. The court arrangement for 30 players shown in Figure 4.1 can be used for this practice.

Postseason Conditioning

During the off-season, players should continue running and also play tennis, handball, squash rackets, or racketball. Because these activities share many similarities with badminton, they support and reinforce badminton skills.

IMPROVING INDIVIDUAL PERFORMANCE

Coaching focuses on the interaction between the coach and the athletes in their mutual attempt to achieve maximum performance and success. Such factors as the organization of practice sessions, team selection, scheduling of matches, and advice on strategy are all responsibilities of the coach.

Organization of Practice Sessions

Daily practice sessions should not exceed three hours; preferably, they should last two hours. Although these sessions should start and stop on time, many players may arrive early and stay late. Thus, the coach must plan to be on the court well in advance of the practice session and stay as long as players seek help. Included in each practice session are warm-up, stroke practice, drills, play, and cool-down.

Since warm-up has been discussed, only one other comment need be made. The coach should decide if players should warm up individually as they arrive or as a team.

During each practice session, every player should hit at least 50 shots to designated target areas. All stroking is done under the supervision of the instructor so that he or she can make corrections if necessary and note areas that need individual help. Strokes can be practiced by pairs hitting together. Because smashing requires extreme exertion, not more than two to three minutes of consecutive action should be permitted.

Drills for use in practice sessions are presented in Chapters 5, 6, and 7. They provide stroke practice in simulated game situations. In all drills the player practicing as a single should be permitted to go full speed for no longer than five minutes at a time. These drills should be general in nature so that all players participate.

Since all players do not share the same strengths or weaknesses, after this general practice each player should practice drills that meet his or her needs. Throughout these drills the coach must supervise players to be sure that movements are performed correctly.

Mixed doubles play has the natural element of men versus women. Thus, men and women can practice all of these badminton drills together. Only smashes pose a potential problem. When practicing the return of smashes hit by a man whose strength is much greater than hers, a woman should first practice returning half-paced smashes. Then the pace should be increased gradually until the man is hitting full strength.

Following the drills, competitive singles and men's, women's, and mixed doubles should be played at full intensity. A limit of three games per practice session should be set. Early season games should pit each student against his or her classmates in singles. In doubles, players should play with and against each other. The results of these games are the basis of the ladder challenge tournaments and team selection.

Team Selection

Ladder challenge tournaments maintain motivation and determine the best players or teams at any given point. Policies for ladder challenges should be established prior to the development of the ladder and followed exactly. A player cannot challenge players who rank more than two rungs above him or her. Once a player has won a position on the team (singles) for two consecutive weeks, he or she must be defeated twice before being displaced.

In selecting doubles teams, the coach either can let players choose their own partners or can pair the players on the basis of their strengths and weaknesses (the approach preferred by this writer). In a team situation the teams should be composed of those who play best together but may not be the best individual players. Therefore, challenges in doubles must be set up on the basis of the different combinations. The changing skill and adjustment levels as well as different temperaments makes the doubles selection more difficult.

Scheduling of Match Play

Match play has two basic components: dual matches and tournaments. The number of dual matches scheduled depends on whether the team is a member of a league in which league policy prevails. When a team is not a member of a league, the number of matches it plays depends on finances and school policy.

Since skill development depends on competition with players of equal or slightly higher caliber, dual matches should be scheduled with teams of equal or better ability. After all, a winning record without individual improvement is not worth the time invested. By this time players should be conditioned to play three games; therefore, they should play at the same pace even when a game seems lost because sometimes continued pressure brings about a turning point. Players should also be counseled to win the first two games whenever possible; this reduces fatigue and maintains players' strength for following matches. All dual matches should be charted and match results used for practice sessions the following week. The coach and the player together should analyze the data and discuss the areas where weaknesses seem to exist. The week's practice schedule is then based on that analysis of strengths and weaknesses.

ARRANGING A TOURNAMENT

Tournament play calls for a somewhat different approach. Since tournament play demands that players sometimes play matches without much rest in between, players must play well enough to win and yet conserve energy. The coach can assist tournament players by keeping up with the draw (schedule of matches and opponents), observing and scouting opponents' play, and then, together with players, outlining tactics for each match. Whether a player warms up with a teammate or with the opponent is a matter of individual preference. (This writer prefers warming up with the opponent.) The most important thing is that the player warms up.

Sponsorship of tournaments provides teams with the opportunity to compete against more experienced players. When a group decides to sponsor a tournament, the following 13 steps should prove helpful:

1. Set a date based on the availability of the desired facility.
2. Obtain permission for the use of the facility. (Steps 1 and 2 should be taken at the same time and about a year in advance of the proposed tournament.)
3. If the sponsoring group is large, a tournament committee can be formed to oversee the operation of the tournament.
4. Form other committees as necessary.
5. Send the proposed date to the United States Badminton Association along with an application or request for approval or sanction.
6. Send notices to all interested parties and arrange for publicity.
7. Contract for shuttles and trophies.
8. Send entry blanks and housing and dining information to all concerned parties.
9. After entries have been returned, prepare the draw.
10. Arrange for officials when necessary.
11. Set up courts for play on day of the tournament.
12. Administer the tournament.
13. Award trophies.

Finally, any person teaching badminton classes should make it a practice not only to talk with other players, coaches, officials, and interested people to get new ideas and discuss techniques and drills but also to watch better players and analyze their performances. Players should also be encouraged to talk with other players and coaches.

Appendix A

Construction of Wooden Standards* for Badminton Court

Wooden standards discussed in Chapter 3 can support the net at the sidelines as well as support the attachments necessary to set up target areas for stroking practice and skill tests. They can be constructed at school. Specifications for three different units follow. The accompanying diagrams are not drawn to scale.

SPECIFICATIONS

Unit A consists of a 1 foot by 1 foot by 1½-inch base with a center pole 5 feet 1¼ inches high. This pole can be made from 1- by 1-inch stock or 1- by ¾-inch stock. A notch ¼ inch deep and ½ inch wide is cut across the top of the pole.

Unit B is made from the same-sized wood stock as that used for Unit A. Two holes are drilled through the wood. The center of the top hole is 1½ inch from the end. The center of the lower hole is 6 inches below the top hole. Thus, the center of the lower hole is 4½ inches from the lower end of the rod.

Attached to this pole is a metal sleeve (B^1) 6 inches long and 1½ inches wide. A long notch 3 inches long and ½ inch wide is cut so that when it is placed over Unit A there is a hole through which the net cord can be passed. When the sleeve is placed over the main pole, both pieces of wood meet. The center of the lowest hole is 6 inches above the net cord.

Unit C is a single piece of wood stock 1⁵/₁₆ inches wide and ½ inch thick. Three holes are drilled in it. The centers of the other two holes are 6 inches apart from the lowest hole, which is ¹¹/₁₆ inch from the end. This bar is attached to Unit B by a bolt and a winged nut.

*These standards were designed and developed by this writer.

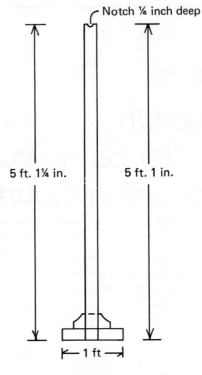

Notch ¼ inch deep

5 ft. 1¼ in.   5 ft. 1 in.

|← 1 ft →|

Unit A

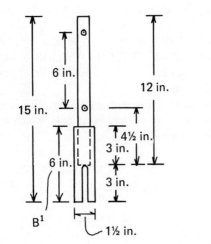

15 in.

6 in.

6 in.

B¹

12 in.

4½ in.

3 in.

3 in.

1½ in.

Unit B

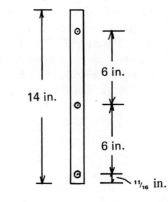

14 in.

6 in.

6 in.

¹¹⁄₁₆ in.

Unit C

Appendix B

Random Selection of Partners and Opponents for Class Badminton Competition

This chart was developed to free the instructor from having to select partners and opponents for class competition. The intent is to have students play five games with one partner and then change partners. This procedure necessitates an adjustment to a new partner, a primary course objective for all levels of badminton instruction.

DOUBLES PLAY

1. List students alphabetically (separate lists for male and female students in a coeducational class) and then assign each student a number (beginning with number 1).
2. Assuming there are 32 male students or 32 female students, the chart is used as follows:

   a. In round 1, students 3 and 16 are paired against 12 and 18. Pairings for the remainder of the round are completed in the same way.
   b. Each team plays one game of five minutes only; the leading team wins no matter what the score.

3. When all games in round 1 are completed, assign a number to each team, e.g., players 3 and 16 become team 1. Now shift to round A, B, C, and D with each team playing the opponent listed.
4. At the conclusion of round D, new pairings are made as indicated in round 2 by repeating steps 2 and 3.

When there are fewer than 32 students in a class, let's say 24, proceed as follows:

1. List students alphabetically.
2. In round 1, cross out all numbers higher than 24.

   a. Students 3 and 16 are paired and play students 12 and 18.
   b. The next two students, 23 and 11, are opposed by students 14 and 20.
   c. The remainder of round 1 is determined in the same way.
   d. When round 1 is completed, select the pairings for round A as described earlier—each team in round A numbered higher than 13 is crossed out and the remainder of round A is paired up.
   e. When round A is completed, schedule new opponents according to the schedule shown in round B.

Chart for Random Selection of Badminton Partners and Opponents

32 Students

Round 1	Round 2	Round 3
3-16 vs 12-18	15-23 vs 28-3	30-22 vs 6-16
26-23 vs 31-27	27-6 vs 7-11	1-29 vs 4-5
29-11 vs 14-20	8-20 vs 10-26	21-25 vs 7-27
5-7 vs 30-17	1-5 vs 14-22	10-26 vs 8-20
9-22 vs 1-21	19-9 vs 30-12	12-31 vs 32-24
8-24 vs 19-25	13-2 vs 21-31	23-15 vs 11-2
28-15 vs 10-4	17-16 vs 4-25	18-17 vs 14-13
13-32 vs 6-2	32-18 vs 24-29	19-3 vs 9-28

Round 4	Round 5
5-30 vs 14-24	9-18 vs 26-7
31-32 vs 23-27	29-15 vs 31-19
2-3 vs 8-7	12-27 vs 3-14
1-22 vs 10-18	25-6 vs 13-24
21-29 vs 20-25	1-22 vs 4-5
28-15 vs 19-6	17-16 vs 11-32
26-16 vs 17-13	8-21 vs 28-2
12-11 vs 4-9	23-10 vs 20-30

Round A	Round B	Round C	Round D
6 vs 12	11 vs 6	11 vs 7	8 vs 6
3 vs 4	4 vs 2	15 vs 6	14 vs 16
10 vs 8	5 vs 9	16 vs 13	2 vs 9
16 vs 5	7 vs 8	1 vs 12	10 vs 7
9 vs 7	10 vs 16	9 vs 5	5 vs 13
13 vs 15	15 vs 14	2 vs 3	15 vs 4
11 vs 2	3 vs 13	10 vs 14	11 vs 1
14 vs 1	12 vs 1	4 vs 8	3 vs 12

When mixed doubles are scheduled, the first number within the class represents the woman and the second number, the man. The opponents are represented by the next two numbers in the schedule.

SINGLES PLAY

When singles are scheduled, each pair of numbers (e.g., 3-16, 12-18) become opponents.

Selected Annotated Bibliography

Books

Bloss, Margaret V. *Badminton.* 4th ed. Brown Physical Education Activities Series. Dubuque, Iowa: William C. Brown Co. Publishers, 1980.

An excellent, comprehensive book designed for physical education classes. Contains historical notes, skills, strategy, self-evaluation questions, glossary of terms, examination questions, and a list of local clubs for the enthusiast. References included.

Davidson, Kenneth R., and Gustavson, Lealand R. *Winning Badminton.* New York: A. S. Barnes and Co., Inc., 1953.

An excellent book covering all aspects of badminton. Photographs and diagrams presented with clarity. Is an easily read text but not readily available.

Finston, Irving L., and Remsberg, Charles. *Inside Badminton.* Chicago: Contemporary Books, Inc., 1978.

A recently published book containing many action photographs. Written in a popular style, it appears to be more suited for experienced players than beginners. Includes some group drills.

Friedrich, John, and Rutledge, A. *Beginning Badminton.* Wadsworth Sports Skills Series. Belmont, California: Wadsworth Publishing Company, Inc., 1962.

One of the early books in the sports skills series. Covers basic fundamentals, singles and doubles play, values, background, and some self-evaluation questions. Bibliography provided.

Jackson, Carl H., and Swan, Lester A. *Better Badminton.* New York: A. S. Barnes and Co., Inc., 1939.

An older but easily read text with good illustrations and diagrams. Not readily available.

Johnson, M. L. *Badminton.* Saunders Physical Activities Series. Philadelphia: W. B. Saunders Company, 1974.

A good book on the fundamentals of the game. Emphasizes mechanics but addresses history, values, and strategy. Contains charts of errors and their causes and methods of correction as well as skills tests. Glossary and bibliography provided.

Official Rules of Play. Swartz Creek, Michigan: United States Badminton Association, 1977.

Presents the official rules of the game with suggestions on the organization of tournaments, the duties of officials, and procedures for arranging the draw.

Poole, James. *Badminton.* Goodyear Physical Activities Series. Pacific Palisades, California: Goodyear Publishing Company, Inc., 1969.

Covers history, equipment, rules, game fundamentals, strategy, and physical conditioning.

Rogers, Wynn. *Advanced Badminton.* Brown Physical Education Activities Series. Dubuque, Iowa: William C. Brown Co., Publishers, 1970.

An excellent text on advanced play. Contains self-evaluation questions and comprehensive sections on strategy. A book any average tournament player should read.

Articles

Bell, Margaret. "Badminton—Getting Started with Power." *Badminton USA* 39 (September 1979): 11-12.

An important article on techniques for developing the power needed for badminton strokes.

Chrisman, Dorothy. "Badminton at 65 and Older." *Journal of Physical Education and Recreation* 50 (October 1979): 26-28.

A very interesting article on the results of a badminton class for women 36 to 78. A discussion of problems, solutions, and teaching aids included.

Davis, P. R. "Speed Is in the Mind." *Badminton Gazette* 58 (November 1976): 50.

One of a series of three articles on improving one's game. For advanced players, it discusses the mental qualities needed to play badminton well.

——. ". . . And in the Feet." *Badminton Gazette* 58 (December 1976): 93.

The second of a three-part series on improving one's game. Provides exercises for improving stamina and footwork for advanced players.

——. "Good Service!" *Badminton Gazette* 58 (March 1977): 184.

The third of a three-part series on improving one's game. Deals with the service and how to make it more effective.

Devlin, J. Frank. "Badminton from the Beginning." *Bird Chatter* 25 (March-April 1966): 14-15.

The first of a series of nine instructional articles on the fundamental skills of badminton. Focuses on the smash, drop, and net shots.

Ibid., 25 (May-June 1966): 22.

The second article in a nine-part instructional series. Covers the low and high service.

Ibid., 26 (November 1966): 21.

The third article of a nine-part series. Covers service variations and the receiving of service.

Ibid., 26 (January 1967): 21-22.

The fourth article in a nine-part instructional series. Deals with the drive.

Ibid., 26 (March 1967): 24.

The fifth article in a nine-part instructional series. Provides the player with procedures for responding to an opponent's smash.

Devlin, J. Frank. "Badminton from the Beginning." *Badminton USA* 27 (November 1967): 22.

The sixth article in a nine-part instructional series. Discusses the singles game and stresses the serve.

Ibid., 27 (January 1968): 16-17.

The seventh article in a nine-part instructional series. Discusses singles play, its strategy and the proper use of certain shots as well as the value of good judgment.

Ibid., 27 (February 1968): 12.

The eighth article in a nine-part instructional series. Outlines the tactical implications and procedures for success in doubles play.

Ibid., 27 (March 1968): 10-11.

The ninth article in a nine-part instructional series. Discusses the strategy of mixed doubles, skills needed by the woman, and the strategy needed when the woman is pulled away from the net.

Devlin, J. Frank. "The Importance of Footwork." *Bird Chatter* 26 (March 1967): 2.

Written by request. Covers in detail the necessity of having good footwork if one wishes to improve his or her game.

Downey, Jake. "An Analysis of the Game." *Badminton USA* 39 (November 1979): 8-9.

An excellent article on competitive situations and appropriate responses (includes a chart) for intermediate and advanced players.

——. "The Uber Cup." *The Badminton Gazette* 56 (December 1974): 78, 100; 56 (February 1975): 132.

An article for top-level competitors or advanced students in which the game is equated with a chess match or a battle. An intellectual endeavor with 12 main points.

Edwards, John. "Putting It Across." *Badminton Gazette* 59 (February 1978): 142.

An excellent article on methods, techniques, and principles of teaching.

Edwards, Marigold A. "Competitive Badminton and Tension Control." *Badminton USA* 40 (January 1980): 13.

A very interesting article on the neuromuscular aspects of the game and the need to voluntarily self-regulate neuromuscular tensions during play, in short, how to "keep cool."

Harvey, Mike. "All England 'Teach In.' " *Badminton Gazette* 59 (November 1977): 59.

A discussion of the psychology and strategy of serving for advanced players.

Hinkle, Phil. "The Paw." *Bird Chatter* 20 (March-April 1961): 5.

Outlines values to be achieved by playing badminton.

Hollocks, Alan. "Four Pillars of Wisdom." *Badminton Gazette* 58 (October 1976): 14.

Stresses the requirements needed to be a champion. Written for highly skilled players.

Johnston, Ray. "Oh Don't Deceive Me." *Badminton Gazette* 56 (March 1975): 158-159.

Discusses advanced shots and deception.

Massman, Bea. "Cause and Effect in Badminton Doubles." *Badminton Gazette* 59 (December 1977): 92.

A fine article on serving and receiving in doubles.

Nelson, Jonathan E. "Teaching Badminton to Groups." *Journal of Physical Education and Recreation* 51 (October 1980): 26-28.

Outlines the "station" concept of instruction for use in a large class.

Norton, Charles. *Catalog of the Louisville Badminton Supply, 1981.* Louisville, Kentucky, Louisville Badminton Supply, 1981.

Poole, James. "The Backhand." *Bird Chatter* 20 (November-December 1960): 11, 20.

Discusses the mechanics of the backhand stroke with drills that help in the development of the stroke.

Rantzmayer, Jurgen. "Wrist Snap—Myth or Reality?" *Badminton Gazette* 58 (February 1977): 128-129.

Deals with James Poole's thesis that power in a stroke is developed by pronation and supination of the forearm rather than by the flexion of the hand at the wrist.

Rogers, Wynn. "Men's Doubles Strategy." *Bird Chatter* 20 (January-February 1961): 13, 21.

The first of two articles on doubles strategy. Discusses the development of offensive strategy.

Ibid., 20 (March-April 1961): 9, 18.

The second of two articles on doubles strategy. Discusses the serve and return of serve and return of serve and defense.

Roper, Peter. "Staying on the Boil." *Badminton Gazette.* 56 (May 1975): 196.

A series of stroking drills and footwork for intermediate, advanced, and competitive players.

Rutledge, Abbie. "Teaching the Adult Beginner." *Bird Chatter* 22 (November-December 1962): 12-13.

A very good article about problems and helpful hints for teaching adult beginners.

Staples, Ev. "Doubles: Serving and Receiving." *Badminton USA* 39 (March 1980): 17-18.

A very good article on the serving and receiving aspects of doubles.

Varner, Margaret. "Ideas for Developing Skill in Badminton." *Bird Chatter* 22 (January-February 1963): 12.

The first of two articles. Contains drills that help players of all skill levels improve their performance.

Ibid., 22 (March-April 1963): 12.

The second of two articles. Outlines drills for developing badminton skills.

Wilkinson, William H. G. "When Hitting Above the Belt Is the Same as Hitting Below the Belt . . . If You See What I Mean." *Badminton Gazette* 58 (March 1977): 162.

An interesting article outlining the factors involved in strategy.

Woolhouse, John. "International Coaching Conference." *Badminton Gazette* 59 (October 1977): 14.

Like the Rantzmayer article, this deals with James Poole's thesis that power in a stroke is developed by pronation and supination of the forearm rather than by the flexion of the hand at the wrist.

Index